Skeptical Guitarist Publications
Catalog

www.SkepticalGuitarist.com

Guitar From Scratch Series

Guitar From Scratch
Meet the Basic Chords * Switching Among Them
Strumming and Fingerpicking * Chord Families
Chord Progressions * Jazz Chords * Barre Chords
Anchor Chords * Power Chords * Pivot Fingers

Guitar From Scratch: The Sequel
Single Notes, Melodies and Scales
Simple Chord Tricks, Licks and Cliches
Learning to Read Just Enough Music

Fingerstyle Guitar From Scratch
Arpeggios and Picking Technique
Travis-Style: The Alternating Bass
Variations and Examples

Blues Guitar From Scratch
Twelve-Bar Blues Structure * Boogie-Woogie
Pentatonic Minor Scale * Blue Notes * Box Patterns
Pentatonic Major Scale * Slide Technique

Travis-Style Guitar From Scratch
Use the Alternating Bass to play fingerstyle solos
Spice up your own arrangements by adding pinches,
syncopation, picking patterns, bass runs and slurs

~ ~ ~ ~ ~ ~ ~ ~ ~ ~ ~

Music Principles for the Skeptical Guitarist Series

Volume One:
The Big Picture
The Layout of the Notes * Chords and Chord Quality
The 1 - 4 - 5 System * The *C-A-G-E-D* Chord Families
The Major Scale * The Key of C in Detail * Worksheets
The Amazing Circle of Fifths * Backcycling * Minor Keys

Volume Two:
The Fretboard
Complex Chord Qualities and Chord Voicings
Working with the Five Chord and Scale Shapes
Moving these Shapes All Around the Neck
Voice Leading * Chord Substitution

Jazz for the Skeptical Guitarist
The 1-6-2-5 Chord Progression * Improvisation
Altered and Extended Dominant Sevenths * Modes

~ ~ ~ ~ ~ ~ ~ ~ ~ ~ ~

Christmas Strumalong Guitar
Lyrics and accompaniment for traditional
carols presented at 2 playing levels

Christmas Fingerstyle Guitar
Instrumental arrangements of traditional
carols presented at 3 playing levels

Comments from Readers

Emery is a teacher who apparently has ESP when it comes to learning guitar. Things are broken down into such sensible pieces that you'll wonder why everybody doesn't teach this way. *Recommended!*
Elderly Instruments, Lansing, MI

Thank you for writing something intelligent and witty, something I actually looked forward to reading. Eternal gratitude.
Meredith Cox, Raleigh, NC

I bought your book because it made me laugh.
Mike Schwartz, Montclair, NJ

Send more books! Our customers are eating them like peanuts.
Linda Tillman, McFadyen Music, Fayetteville, NC

Thanks for your warm and friendly style and bits of humorous illustration.
George Demosthenes, New Market, NH

Focused and vastly readable... Conversational approach is warm and engaging...Humor, insight and patience.
David McCarty, Acoustic Guitar Magazine

You are a miracle worker. I'm having the time of my life.
Chuck Slaughter, Cyberspace

The books sell themselves.
David Willmott, Music-Go-Round, Cary, NC

It's written just like you're sitting there teaching me.
Barrett Ferrara, Cyberspace

Your writing is breezy and conversational but still very clear and organized.
Chris Gaskill, Knoxville, TN

You clearly have a real gift, and we're lucky that you put it down on paper
Mark Waite. Houston, TX

There is no better teaching aid on the market than your books. You could write a book on the proper way to put a guitar on a guitar stand and I would buy it! **Kevin Johnson, San Antonio, TX**

The format is easy on the eyes. Bruce writes in a clear and understandable manner, making it fun to learn.
Ed Benson, Just Jazz Guitar magazine

If you write it, they will buy it.
Paul Miller, New Bern, NC

Bruce, this is an absolutely terrific book. It shows that you have a wonderful sense of humor, a high degree of humility and a great sensitivity to others. A++ and many kudos.
Dick Masom, Tequesta, FL

Bruce Emery has "got it right" with his gentle pace.
Adrian Ingram, Just Jazz Guitar magazine

I can see why people raved about this. This is a great thing you did.
Thomas McLachlen, Pittsburgh, PA

Your content is golden.
Marko Schmitt, Cyberspace

Thanks for getting me fired up! I can play more in 4 weeks than I could after all those years of trying to teach myself.
Kim Lachance, Dover, NH

Your books are greatness because of the enjoyment you experienced while writing them. I was instantly won over by your wit.
Christian Briere, Weatherford, TX

Enjoyable to read; short, to the point and jam-packed full of information.
Lynn Sugg, Winterville, NC

All I can say is YES! Someone has finally hit the nail on the head.
Martin Bell, Staffordshire, England

$16.50

Companion Audio Tracks available at: www. SkepticalGuitarist .com

Fingerstyle Guitar From Scratch

The purpose of this book is to get you familiar with
Fingerstyle Vocal Accompaniment.

Instead of strumming chords with a pick to back up your singing voice
(or some other instrument), you'll be using your fingers to pick individual notes
out of those chords. It's just a kinder, gentler way to play rhythm guitar.

Think of "Dust in the Wind," "Scarborough Fair," "Landslide,"
"Leader of the Band," "Time in a Bottle."

It CAN, however, lead to what they call **Solo Fingerstyle Guitar**,
where a melody line is woven into the fabric of the chordal accompaniment,
as in classical style, blues, jazz, Celtic folk music and the styles of
Chet Atkins, Merle Travis and many other instrumentalists.
That will come in future publications.

Classical methods start out teaching you to play single note melody lines,
and if you would feel more comfortable with that angle, there are many fine
method books available, such as Aaron Shearer's *Classic Guitar Technique.*
I studied the Shearer method myself, but now I happen to feel that
the chordal approach leads to quicker results
because it's more fun.

So, lose that triangular plastic thingy,
limber up those little sausages and
Let's Fingerpick!

Fingerstyle Guitar From Scratch

by

Bruce Emery

Skeptical Guitarist Publications

www.SkepticalGuitarist.com

© Copyright 2003 Skeptical Guitarist Publications

All rights reserved; no part of this publication may be reproduced, stored in a retrieval system, or transmitted, in any form or by any means, electronic, mechanical, photocopying, recording, or otherwise, without the prior written permission of Skeptical Guitarist Publications.

Manufactured in the United States of America

ISBN: 0-9665029-6-5
ISBN: 978-0-9665029-6-1

Cover design: Marc Harkness   <harkness@bellsouth.net>
Webmaster: Lou Dalmaso   <loudalmaso@aol.com>

Skeptical Guitarist Publications
P. O. Box 5824
Raleigh, NC 27650-5824
(919) 834-2031

Web site: www.skepticalguitarist.com
Find audio files and an e-mail link

Second Edition

Table of Contents

The Fingerstyle F Chord.............................1

Part One: Fingerstyle Basics...................2

Notation...3

The Picking Hand...............................4

Picking Philosophies..........................5

The Overlapping Tier System................6

The Fretting Hand.............................7

Bass/Tier Combinations.....................8

Practice with Arpeggio #1...................9

The Continuity Principle....................12

The Indiana Jones Principle................13

More Examples................................14

Worst-Case Continuity Scenario............17

The Challenge.................................19

Other Meters: 3/4 Time......................20

Other Meters: 6/8 Time......................22

Back to 4/4 Time: "Estudio".................24

Meet the Twins................................26

Other Simple Arpeggios: "Pachelbel".....27

Arpeggios with Longer Sequences..........29

"Allegro"..31

3/3/2 Time......................................32

20 Arpeggios: A Retrospective..............34

Mixing Quarter and Eighth Notes..........35

Meet the Trio...................................36

More Samples from the Field................37

Game Show: "Scarborough Fair"...........38

"Time in a Bottle"..............................40

Bossa Nova: "Girl From Ipanema".........42

Part Two: Travis-Style Basics.....................44

Travis #1: Inside-Out...........................45

Mechanics......................................46

Practice: "City of New Orleans"...............47

Travis #2: "Landslide"...........................49

Travis #3: Outside-In..........................51

Variations: Travis #4 and #5.................52

Picking Pattern Potpourri....................53

Triple Alternating Bass........................54

Walking Bassline...............................56

Travis #6: The Pinch Pattern.................57

"Dust in the Wind".............................58

Pinch Variations...............................62

Adding the Ring Finger.......................64

Drop D and the Ring Finger.................65

More "Landslide" Variations.................66

Jerry Reed Picking Pattern...................67

20 Travis Patterns: A Retrospective.........68

"Leader of the Band...........................69

"Garden Party".................................72

Double-Picking.................................74

"Helplessly Hoping"...........................75

Travis-Style Departures......................76

"The Dance"....................................77

"Blackbird".....................................78

The Next Level: Melodic Lines..............85

Final Exam......................................87

Our 20 Arpeggios at a Glance..............88

Our 20 Travis Pattern at a Glance.........89

Big sloshing buckets of gratitude go to
my strongest fingerstyle guitar influences:

Joanne Ryan
Eric Schoenberg
James Taylor
John Knowles
Jerry Reed
Chet Atkins
and
Pierre Bensusan

First, a Word About..... *The Fingerstyle F Chord*

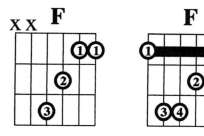

When I began playing guitar, I learned that there were two ways to play the F chord in 1st position. They are known by their nicknames, Horrible and Horribler:

Since then, I have stumbled upon two other ways that are considered by the classical guitar world to be unorthodox at best and Evil at worst.

It's the thumb, fretting the F note on the 6th string, that throws people into a dither.

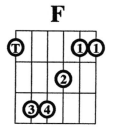 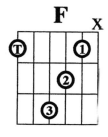

My guess is that all the outrage and carrying on stems from a simple misunderstanding on the part of the Father of the Modern Classical Guitar, Andres Segovia. Here's my theory: Segovia started his musical career as a violinist, and when you play the violin, you keep your left thumb behind the neck, not curled around the fingerboard. There is probably a good reason for keeping the thumb back there, but I'll leave that to the violinists.

Anyway, so my theory goes, Segovia arbitrarily carried this practice over to the guitar and adhered to it dogmatically, despite the fact that the fingerings for some very nice chord voicings are being kept out of our reach, such as:

Ideology can negate both beauty and practicality.

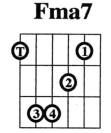 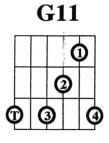

To be sure, there are situations where the thumb is needed behind the neck, as in playing barre chords, where the clamping action is necessary for articulating all the notes. But my usual left hand position has the thumb hanging over the fretboard, the neck comfortably cradled in the palm of my hand. Whenever I need to play a barre chord, I drop my wrist, swing my thumb to the back of the neck and straighten out my 1st finger for the barre, no problem. Some might say I should keep my wrist in the dropped position all the time; those same people might recommend that I wear a raincoat even when it's not raining.

It may take a little stretching for you to get these thumbed F chords working. I didn't start doing it until I'd been playing the guitar for ten years, and it sure seemed like an annoyance to learn to do, but the need was there. It certainly has made me a more versatile player, and that is sort of the whole point.

Part One: Fingerstyle Basics

Fingerstyle Guitar is my favorite musical pastime. You don't have to ask me twice to play Fingerstyle Guitar. You know those other five books I wrote? Did 'em just to get 'em out of the way so I could spend the rest of my life writing about Fingerstyle.

You *don't* know about those other five books? No matter. I'll refer to them once in a while, but it's not like you'll be hopelessly lost if you haven't read them. *"Scratch"* and the *"Sequel"* go into chord basics, some single note stuff and a primer on reading Standard Music notation ("the notes"), and *"SkepGuit One,"* *"Two"* and *"Three"* talk about the theory of Chord Families, chord and scale positions around the neck and the basics of blues and jazz.

The focus here will be coordinating the **Picking Hand** (usually the right hand) with the **Fretting Hand** (usually not the right hand), so I'll assume that you are comfortable with chord formation and some theory. If you are not, then you might consider throwing good money after bad and acquiring some of my other books.

One of them, *Guitar From Scratch,* contains a more cursory treatment of fingerstyle technique that might just suffice. You also might want to look ahead to page 34 of this book ("Twenty Arpeggios") to see an overview of some of the more important picking patterns.

I played the guitar for 5 years before I dared to lay the flatpick aside. Actually, I was forced into it, gently, by my favorite guitar teacher, Joanne Ryan. *And it felt like I was starting to play guitar all over again!* It felt weird, and it may for you, too. But since playing fingerstyle turns out to be my favorite way to play, I wish I had been exposed to it earlier.

I also wish I hadn't spent 10 years of my life studying forestry, but that's spilt milk over the dam.

Then again, by the time I met Joanne, I had the Fretting Hand *down pat* and I really shot through the book I was using (Aaron Shearer's *Classic Guitar Technique*) because I could focus mainly on the Picking Hand. But even if you're relatively new to the guitar, there's no reason why you shouldn't try playing fingerstyle right now.

Okay. **Fingernails.** It's not *necessary* to use them. In earlier days, people played with just the tips of their fingers. It wasn't until that crazy Spaniard Andres Segovia came along that fingernails became cool. Segovia's concern was for the music to be heard throughout the concert hall, and fingernails improved the attack and pumped up the volume. (He went so far as to station someone outside the main door of the concert hall to shush the passersby.)

So fingernails are desirable, but some people just can't keep them. You can experiment with different kinds of fingerpicks and thumbpicks. Classical players eschew them (bless you!). Nashville players use just a thumbpick. Some folks get all decked out with a pick on every finger, while others say that if you use any kind of pick at all, you erect a barrier between yourself and "the music." (I doubt it.)

There's also a technique called **hybrid picking**, where you hold a flatpick between Thumb and Index finger and then add the Middle and Ring fingers. In a way, I am envious of people who can do this, and I guess I could learn to do it myself, because there are advantages. But, as with many things in life, there are also disadvantages. I've just stuck with the unadorned Thumb-and-three-finger approach that is consistent with my classical training.

So we'll proceed using the **Thumb, Index, Middle** and **Ring fingers** of the Picking Hand. (What about the Pinky? Well, the classical players don't use it, but once in a while it *can* help out, so let's keep it "on hand.")

And we'll rely on our old friend, the **Tablature** (or **Tab**) **Diagram** to show *which* finger is to play *what* string and *when*. I am caught here between the classical and folk philosophies of fingerstyle guitar. I love using Tab (classical players do not) because it is so explicit and takes the guesswork out of which note to play. Reading "the notes" is useful for the purposes of music theory and composition, but that is not our concern here. We need to get you playing as soon, and with as few impediments, as possible.

As I mentioned in the Introduction, the scope of this book is to give you some fingerpicking patterns with which you can accompany your own voice or some other source of melody. Trying to *incorporate* that melody into the patterns *themselves* is the next step up, and that will come in future publications.

So for now we'll consider a picking pattern to be composed of two elements: the **bass note**, usually played by the Thumb, and the **treble notes**, which usually belong to the fingers. Let's label the fingers of the Picking Hand **p**, **i**, **m** and **a**, in accordance with classical guitar tradition (from Spanish):

It's time to interpret some *diagrams* (below, right). The Fretboard Diagram (the grid) shows you what the Fretting Hand is doing (nothing here) and the Tab Diagram, below it, shows you what the Picking Hand is doing.

p for Thumb *(pulgar)*
i for Index finger *(indice)*
m for Middle finger *(medio)*
a for Ring finger *(anular)*

The Tab tells you to play the 6th string with the Thumb, then play the 3rd string with the Index finger, the 2nd string with the Middle finger and the 1st string with the Ring finger. Try doing this over and over for a bit, keeping the notes evenly spaced in time (rat-tat-tat-tat). You are playing what is known as an **arpeggio**, a (h)**arp**-like broken chord. This particular arpeggio is known as an Ascending Arpeggio because we're moving from lower- to higher-pitched notes.

Let's call this ***Arpeggio #1***, stirring within you the expectation that more arpeggios will follow.

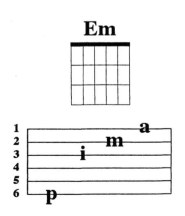

Several points of order are in order:

(1) The Thumb picks *downward* and the fingers pick *upward*.

(2) Lay all 4 fingers down on the assigned strings before you even *think* of making a stroke. This is called **planting**. It's just a nice feeling to have all the piggies lined up in a row before making your move. On the other hand, if the notes in a prior arpeggio are still ringing, postpone planting for the next chord for as long as you can.

(3) Keep your hand *cupped* and make sure you have contact between the strings and your actual fingertips, not just the nails. Try to catch a bit of the nail as you go by. Ponk. Repeat the pattern, striving for an even rhythm.

(4) This one's a biggie: *The hand should not bounce around!* The fingers should move while the hand stays as *motionless* as possible. Most of the finger movement should come from the middle joint.

(5) You need *follow-through*. I don't play golf, but I do know that when you swing the club to hit the ball, you shouldn't jerk it back right after contact is made; you should follow-through. After you strike the string, let your finger curl a bit into your palm, and don't re-extend the finger until just before the next stroke.

(6) Keep your Thumb out *in front* of your Index finger, toward the neck, so they don't bump into each other. They should be able to swing freely past each other.

Point (6) needs some amplification. When sitting to play, most people rest the guitar on the right thigh. But in classical playing, you rest the guitar on the *left thigh* between the legs, with a little footstool under the left foot to give some elevation. Try it. (Of course, if you play the guitar left-handed, this is all reversed.)

Now wait, there's a valid reason for assuming this posture: The neck of the guitar gets tilted upward, so when you lay your Picking Hand across the strings, your fingers approach them at a right angle, and the Thumb *naturally* extends past the fingers. The right angle approach also helps you hit the strings dead on.

Now put the guitar back over your right thigh. See how the neck drops down and your fingers approach the strings at an oblique angle? Now you're more likely to have traffic problems between your Thumb and Index finger, or in the extreme case, the Thumb will swing past the fingers and get swallowed into the palm. And your nails will *scrape*, not pluck.

If you prefer to sit in the classical form, more power to you. As for myself I tried but could never become comfortable sitting that way. So I keep the guitar on the right thigh and *rotate the wrist clockwise* a tad so that I can maintain both the right angle to the strings and the protruding Thumb. I've said my piece. You may now go forth and posture as you will. *Oh, and keep the Thumb straight!*

So. If I'm watching you fingerpick the guitar, I'm seeing: (1) the fingers perpendicular to the strings.....(2) the hand steady, only the fingers in motion..... (3) the Thumb straight.....and (4) the face, the epitome of grim determination.

Now. Looking at that **Em** chord diagram, you might say, Hey, that's no **Em** chord! It's just open strings! Well, a chord is not a chord until you decide *which strings to play.* If you were strumming this chord, yes, you'd need to hold the 4th and 5th strings at the 2nd fret, or it would sound crummy.

But that's the beauty of fingerpicking. Just *don't play* the 4th and 5th strings and you've got yourself a pretty chord.

Notice the "o" over the 6th string in the Chord Diagram, which is a way to emphasize the need to play an open note in the bass of a chord.

Here is where the classical player and the folk player tend to part company. (And by folk player I mean someone who plays folk, rock, pop or country; someone who plays the music of the people, man.) *An argument can be made for holding down the notes on those two strings* ***anyway.*** Here's a typical exchange between a classical player and a folk player, the kind you hear every day, regarding this issue of Stealth Fretting:

Classical Player:	*Well, if I'm playing only the open strings from an Em chord, then I don't need the services of the fretting hand.*
Folk Player:	*Yes, but what if you* ***mistakenly*** *hit one of those other two strings? Don't you want to be covered?*
Classical Player:	*I practice 4 hours a day. I don't make mistakes.*
Folk Player:	*But what if you decide to improvise and play one of those strings* ***intentionally.*** *Don't you want to be prepared?*
Classical Player:	*I don't improvise. I play only the notes that the composer intended for me to play.*

That's right, classical players are known to be deliberate and precise (uptight) while folk players tend to be more casual and adventurous (slobs). I myself bounce back and forth between the two philosophies, sort of an uptight slob. Sometimes I labor neurotically over the sound of a single note and other times I exemplify why they call the guitar an "axe" by hacking my way through great swaths of musical underbrush.

And when I'm in Machete Mode, I hold down ***complete chords*** in the event that I either (1) hit an "unintended" note (screw up) or (2) decide to improvise a bit by choosing alternate strings to play, sort of loosening my grip on the reins of power and allowing to come out what ***wants*** to come out. The classical player has a different agenda, based on a more deferential attitude toward the composer's work, that is, frankly, commendable, despite the bit of fun we've had at his expense. (He isn't reading this book anyway.)

The Overlapping Tier System

Sounds like some kind of crop rotation method. But, in fact, it is a term that I have invented all by myself, without checking with anybody, to describe the way that the fingers of the Picking Hand should be deployed across the strings of the guitar.

As we've already seen, the Thumb, **p**, is generally responsible for playing the three Bass Strings (6th, 5th and 4th), while the three fingers, **i**, **m** and **a**, are assigned to the three Treble Strings (3rd, 2nd and 1st, respectively). This is how we played our **Em** arpeggio.

But it turns out that it's just as common for the fingers to be shifted *up* one string in elevation, or *down* one string in pitch, so that **i** is stationed on the *4th* string, **m** on the *3rd* string and **a** on the *2nd* string. Then **p** plays the 6th and 5th strings.

So we will find our fingers assigned to either one of two overlapping sets, or *tiers*, of strings. In other words, fingers **i**-**m**-**a** will find themselves assigned, in that order, to either strings **3-2-1** or **4-3-2**. I'd like to call the **3-2-1** placement the **Higher Tier** (higher with regard to the pitch of the strings, not their distance from the center of the planet) and the **4-3-2** placement the **Lower Tier**.

To play the **Em** chord in the Lower Tier, you'll actually have to do some work with the Fretting Hand, because that 4th string is now needed. How much work you do depends on whether you feel like wearing the classical or the folk hat, and I give you the two main possible fingerings to the right:

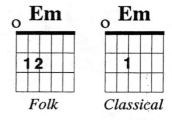

Now, we're trying to adhere to a very important basic tenet:
Adjacent fingers should be assigned to adjacent strings.

It would be a mistake to let just any finger play any old string that it wanted to. Chaos would surely reign and the strong (**i** and **m**) would push aside the weak (**a**).

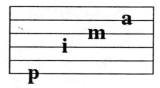

We still call this **Arpeggio #1**, simply the Lower Tier.

When you start flying across the strings, you don't want there to be any doubt as to which finger is in charge of which string. Keep the fingers lined up and move them as a unit when switching between tiers.

There also exists what we may as well call the **Low-Low Tier**, where the three fingers line up on strings **5-4-3** and the Thumb takes the 6th string. This doesn't happen very often; not too many chords sound particularly good down in their nether regions (**Em** does.)

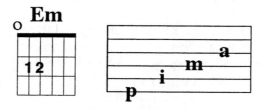

Folk and classical players finally agree!

Here Comes the Fretting Hand

Time to coordinate the activities of the Picking and Fretting Hands, a little like patting your cranium and rubbing your thorax at the same time. The key to this is for the Picking Hand to learn to do its job almost *mindlessly* so that you can do most of your thinking about the Fretting Hand. Of the two hands, the Fretting Hand has the more complicated job, considering all the possible chords and chord fragments that exist on the fretboard, so we have a better chance of getting the Picking Hand to learn to operate on autopilot. So let's get the Picking Hand going in a picking pattern and then challenge it by sneaking in some Fretting Hand activity.

Start with the open **Em** chord, 6th-string bass, Higher Tier, and play the following series of Ascending Arpeggios:

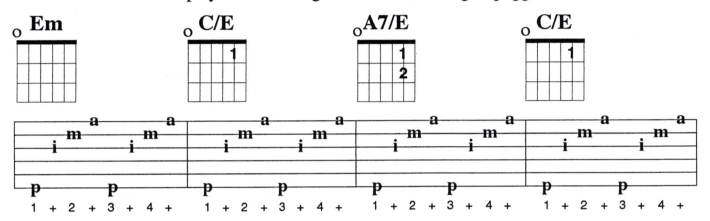

Once you get the Picking Hand going, you can "forget" about it as you turn your attention to the notes being added to the fretboard.

There are two arpeggios per measure for each chord. Across the bottom of the Tab Diagram you see the numbers "1 + 2 + 3 + 4 +," telling you that the Time Signature is **4/4**, meaning that there are 4 strong beats per measure. But there are actually *8 slots* where notes can appear. The "+" signs show where the half-beats are, and in this Picking Pattern we are indeed using all 8 slots, and are therefore playing *8 Eighth Notes* per measure.

Look at what's happened in the **A7/E** chord: We've left the 1st finger on and just added the 2nd. This illustrates another great principle from classical playing: ***Once a finger is down, leave it there until you NEED to remove it.*** Of course, you may need to remove it immediately, but if you don't, leave it there in case you can use it in the next move. That's exactly what happens here, as we're moving back to the same chord we just came from. The presence of the 1st finger has no audible effect in the **A7/E**, since it's being overridden by the 2nd finger.

For you folk players, here are the full chords that you could have held down. Seems pointless, though, *if* you had intended to play only the notes indicated. The 2nd finger would have stayed in place during the chord changes as a Pivot Finger, even though you wouldn't have *played* that note. (The "E" after the slash means that an E note (6th string) appears in the bass of the C and A7 chords.)

Bass/Tier Combinations

Now we'll add in the 5th-string bass, and try a new chord progression. We'll practice it twice, once in the Higher Tier and once in the Lower Tier, resulting in four "Bass/Tier" combinations. Notice that we're holding the bare minimum of notes according to which tier we are assigned.

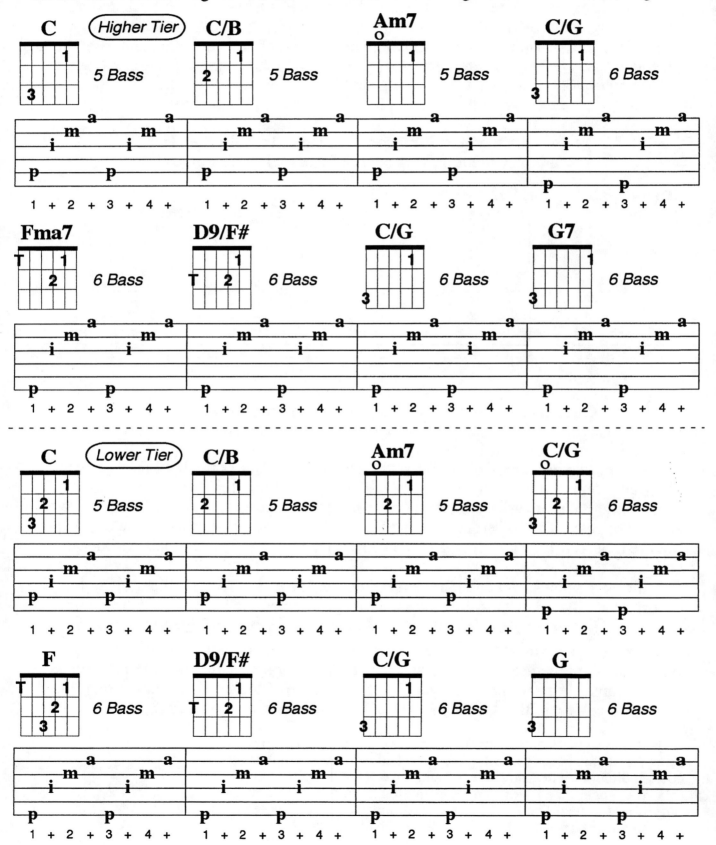

Most chords work well on either the Higher or the Lower Tier. But some chords, namely the plain **D** chord, the baby **F** and the baby **Bb**, have a 4th-string bass occupied by the Thumb, leaving only the Higher Tier for the fingers. Nowhere else to go:

**4th-String Bass
Higher Tier**

You know, there is an almost unlimited number of different sorts of arpeggios that we can play, and I do intend to show you more of them as we go along. So far, we've only looked at one, an ascending pattern with 4 Eighth Notes. But it might be a mistake to throw too many different logs on the fire at once.

My view is that you take a simple pattern and play it until you get wear it out, which should mean that you've got it going on autopilot. Take a bite, chew and swallow, and *then* take another bite. So I want to give you some more practice with this simple pattern. It's a great ***default pattern***, one you won't need to think too much about when you're singing. *As you learn new patterns, feel free to go back to the chords on page 8 and give them a go.*

We'll use the chord progressions from two songs popularized by Alison Krauss and Union Station. **I can't use the words or melodies to copyrighted material**, but you'll get the idea. The pattern for "Now That I've Found You" stays in the Higher Tier while the Thumb roams around in the bass. Try it a couple of times, then we'll talk about it:

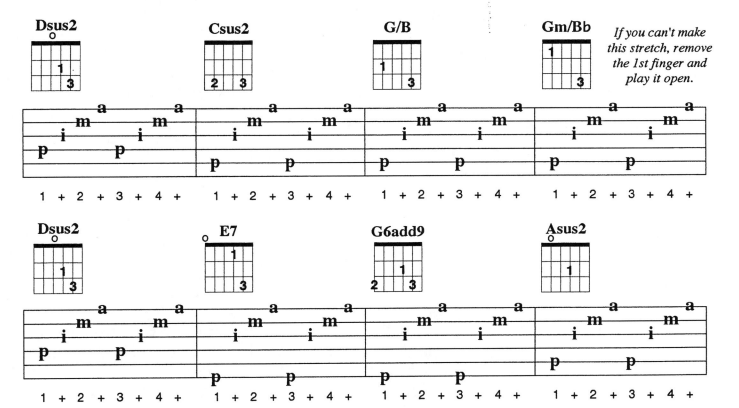

I like teaching that chord progression for several reasons:

(1) It's really rather easy to play for how good it sounds (sorry about the stretch from **G/B** to **Gm/Bb**). The chord changes are minimal and the 3rd finger acts as an *Anchor Finger* all the way until the last measure, when the 1st finger takes over as the Anchor Finger, so every chord is *connected* to the one before and after it.

(2) The open 1st string is allowed to ring continuously, and we like *continuously ringing strings* because they cover our tracks as we move from chord to chord. This is a critical concept in fingerpicking, but let's postpone that discussion until we hit an example where it's *not* so easy to keep strings ringing.

(3) With regard to the Picking Hand, *the fingers are not permitted to follow the Thumb,* as they might like to do. For example, in switching from **Dsus2** to **Csus2**, as the Thumb switches from the 4th- to the 5th-string bass, most people feel the urge to shift the fingers from the Higher to the Lower Tier in pursuit of the Thumb. Uh-uh.

We must establish independence between the fingers-acting-as-a-unit and the Thumb. The fingers must remain rivetted to the Higher Tier and the Thumb must be free to play whichever of the three bass notes is needed Back when you learned to strum, you had to establish **independence** between the two hands. Here the independence must exist *within the Picking Hand itself.*

(4) Dig those partial chords, particularly the **E7** and the **Asus2**. You hold down only as much as you need to, not a single string more. The 1st finger acts as a *Guide Finger*, sliding down from **Dsus2** (2nd fret) to **E7** (1st fret) and then back up to **G6add9** (2nd fret), never losing contact with the string. It gets no better than this.

The other Alison Krauss number I like to use is "When You Say Nothing At All," by Keith Whitley. The Main Riff contains three simple chords spread over two measures, four arpeggios in all, but this time there's more jumping around for the Picking Hand.

Dsus2: We start with 4th-String Bass/Higher Tier. Why the unusual chord fingering? Because you can simply add the 1st finger to form...

Asus4: In this case, the fingers *do* chase the Thumb, with the 5th-String Bass/Lower Tier. Keep the 3rd finger as the Anchor Finger as you go into...

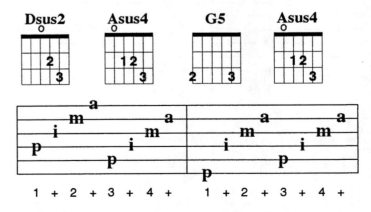

G5: Here, the fingers stay on the Lower Tier as the Thumb moves to the 6th-String Bass, then keep the Lower Tier again as the Thumb returns to the 5th-String Bass for the **Asus4**. In terms of keeping strings ringing, the 2nd string rings over into each new chord since the Anchor Finger never moves. The 1st string rings, too, as long as you don't kill it.

More Fretting Hand Notation

So far, we've been presenting only Picking Hand information in the Tab Diagrams. Another way to use Tab is to give *Fretting Hand* information, such as which fret you should hold down to produce some note in some chord. So instead of the **p-i-m-a**'s, we'll place *the number of the desired fret on the line for the desired string* in the Tab Diagram. So our last example, "**When You Say Nothing at All**," becomes:

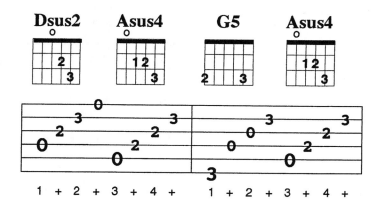

Adding more numbers can add more confusion, so you need to keep it clear that the numbers in the Tab Diagrams are the *fret* numbers, while the numbers in the Fretboard Diagrams are the *finger* numbers of the Fretting Hand.

(Think of it this way: There is no such thing as a "0" finger.)

A complaint may be that the fingerings for the *Picking Hand* are no longer being shown. True, but by now, you should be able to figure out how the **p-i-m-a**'s should be lined up: *You always reserve the Thumb for the **bassest** note in the chord and then assign the other three fingers to three adjacent strings, Higher or Lower Tier.*

Here's what I'll do. I'll keep enlarging the Thumb notes, as above, to keep them distinct. I'll also place tiny little **p-i-m-a**'s just above the Tab if it's not obvious which fingers to use. And the Chord Diagrams are here to stay. I mean, I could omit them and force you to figure out the Fretting Hand fingerings for yourself from the Tab, but that seems kinda mean. Besides, the better fingerings aren't always so obvious, like that **Dsus2** above. So, in the interests of world peace, I'll keep furnishing Chord Diagrams.

- -

Maybe you can guess, what with the enhancement of our notation, that things are about to get more interesting for the Fretting Hand. By now, a simple arpeggio has begun to take root somewhere in your muscle memory, so we can now afford to turn our attention more to the machinations of the Fretting Hand. No longer will we shield it from the harsh reality that it is going to have to do *some work*.

One of the most vital aims in fingerstyle guitar is to *keep the strings ringing*, guys, to squeeze as much juice as we can out of each note we play. It's almost a sacred quest. We strive for **continuity**, or at least the *semblance* of continuity. So far, we've relied on open strings and Anchor Fingers to achieve continuity, but we won't always have them.

For lack of a more imaginative nomenclature, let's call this the **Continuity Principle**. *Both hands will share responsibility for, and contribute to, the furtherance of this quest.*

The Continuity Principle

The problem with the guitar is that, once you strike a note, the sound decays rapidly. Luckily, the successive notes in an arpeggio overlap with each other, so we don't get a dead space between them (assuming we play cleanly). The gap is bridged for free.

But we need to pay more attention to the continuity issue during *chord changes*. We're covered if the last note in the arpeggio (1) is an open string that can ring through, or (2) belongs to the next chord, too, and an Anchor Finger can bridge the gap. But quite often, the last note is a fretted note that needs to be removed because it *doesn't* appear in the next chord. **To imply continuity, you must keep holding that note for its full duration.** No fair leaving early. If you do, you'll leave a gap in the music that EVERYONE will hear.

Of course, this means that there may be almost *zero* time to get to the *next* note. ***Actually, this isn't so bad if you can get to the next note with a different finger,*** which will often be the case. Take a look at this next example involving the transitions between the **G** and **C** chords in both Higher and Lower Tiers.

(The bracketed numbers correspond to the comments below. Dashed lines show transitions.)

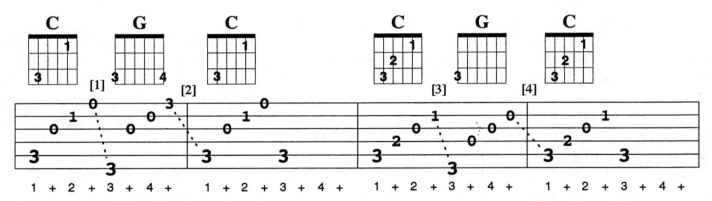

[1] From the **C** to the **G** chord in the Higher Tier, the Continuity Principle is satisfied easily: Just keep that open 1st string (the "0") ringing at least until the start of the G chord on Count 3.

[2] From the **G** back to the **C** chord in the Higher Tier, we run into our first potential continuity problem: That "3" on the 1st string (Count 4+) must keep ringing until the start of the C chord. The 4th finger must stay down long enough to bridge the gap.

[3] From **C** to **G** in the Lower Tier, it's the 1st finger that must stick around to bridge the gap.

[4] From **G** back to **C** in the Lower Tier, it is smooth sailing due to the open 2nd string.

Here's an interesting question: ***Exactly when* do we take away those finger bridges?** We invoke the **Diversion Principle**, which states that the best time to remove a finger from an old note is at the *very same time* that we start a *new* note. Whenever we let go of a note, we take the risk of creating a tiny but unseemly *ping* as a byproduct. Starting a new note can mask that ping, providing *cover* for the old note to get away.

When the hidden assassin in the concert hall depends on the climactic cannon blasts in the *1812 Overture* to mask the report of his revolver, he is using the Diversion Principle.

As long as we're introducing principles, here's one that will ease some of the pressure that we've placed on the Fretting Hand to maintain continuity: the **Indiana Jones Principle**.

At the beginning of *The Raiders of the Lost Ark*, as that huge boulder was bearing down on our hero, it hit me. No, I mean I had an epiphany. As long as Indiana stayed just a fraction of an inch ahead of that boulder, he was safe. He didn't need to be *way* ahead of the boulder, just far enough ahead to avoid getting conked on the noggin.

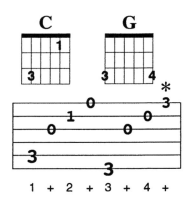

Naturally, this got me thinking about guitar. To the right is the first measure of our last example. When the time comes to switch from the **C** to the **G**, it is clear from the Tab that there is no hurry to set down the *entire* G chord at once. Sure, we need the 3rd finger right away because our Picking Pattern requires that note first. But we don't really need the *4th* finger until 3 notes later (asterisk). Just don't be any later than *that.*

We count on the Picking Hand to play the role of the ruthless, unstoppable boulder, keeping the arpeggio rolling, and yes, the Fretting Hand must remain at least a step ahead of that boulder. Just don't expect to get any extra points by staying *way* ahead.

If you rush *all* of your fingers into the notes of a new chord at once, you risk missing some of your targets. Adding them in sequence, as needed, allows for a more careful placement.

Before we go on, let me say a word about all these little niggling details that I'm always harping on about when to change fingers from chord to chord. There is a good chance that you yourself would come up with a lot of this technique on your own, over time, through trial and error. My aim is to minimize the stumbling around and to steer you away from bad habits and toward good ones so that you'll get to enjoy playing Fingerstyle Guitar sooner. That is all.

In that spirit, and in view of our new principles, let's go back and re-examine the fingerings for "**When You Say Nothing at All.**" Remember to start with that odd fingering for **Dsus2**.

[1] After the **Dsus2** ends with an open string ringing (good cover), the **Asus4** starts with an open string. Well, instead of stampeding the 1st finger into position at the start of the **Asus4** on Count 3, we wait until we really need it on Count 3+, mindful of the boulder.

[2] Here we get a diversion, where the 1st and 2nd fingers (circled) are removed just as the last note in the arpeggio is initiated. Cover those pings!

[3] Another diversion, as the 2nd finger (circled) is removed from the **G** chord.

[4] We re-place the 1st and 2nd fingers (first the 1st finger, then the 2nd), once again keeping ourselves just ahead of the boulder.

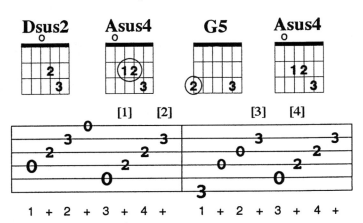

Don't worry, we won't continue to scrutinize *every* chord change from here to eternity. I just want you to see that the process of changing chords can be more fluid and stepwise, and less a matter of just plunking down prefabricated chord forms, one after the other.

Here's a more extended example showing an accompaniment for the song "**The Rose.**" Pay special attention to the notes marked with an asterisk; they must be consciously held until *the start of the next note* to bridge the gap and maintain the feeling of continuity:

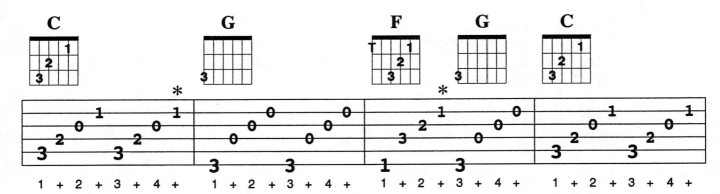

The **2nd line** is the same as the **1st line**, so play it again. All Lower Tier, pretty straightforward. This is the first Fingerstyle **F** that you need to play *in rhythm*; in other words, *on the fly*. First get the thumb (**T**) into position. Now, you could apply the Indiana Jones Principle here and add the fingers in the sequence 3-2-1, but since the three fingers are available anyway, I'd just plop them down all at once (Count 1+).

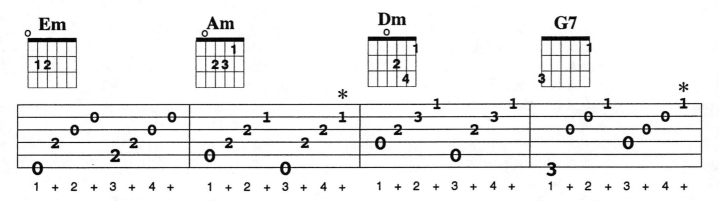

In the **3rd line**, above, we spread our wings. We add alternate basses for all four chords, and we get them for free, since they are already present in the chords. The Root Notes (E for **Em**, A for **Am**, D for **Dm**, G for **G7**) are played first, then come the alternates.

In the case of the **Dm** chord, the 4th string is the Root, so to keep the arpeggio intact, we must shift to the Higher Tier. And once we're in the Higher Tier, we might as well stay there for the **G7** chord, starting with the 6th-string bass. Actually, were we to shift back to the Lower Tier right away, we'd miss the note that makes **G7** a **G7** (F on the 1st string).

And take a look at the Chord Diagram for **Dm**. Though it isn't necessary, it makes sense to use the 4th finger because it was *not* in use during the **Am**. Then at the end of the **Dm**, the 3rd finger is already free and can go right for the 6th string in **G7**. Get the piggies to share.

Then the **4th line** is a repeat of the **1st line**, back in the Lower Tier.

More Examples Using Arpeggio #1

It wouldn't be a terrible thing at this point to just skim through the Tab for a while, playing the examples and ignoring the detailed explanations. Some of the points made in the text may not matter to you until you've been playing the patterns for some time. And feel free to skip ahead and take a look at the Twenty Arpeggios on page 34.

See what you can do with a sequence of chords that I use for the Beatles' **"Yesterday."** It's in the **Key of C**, which suits my voice, and it's all Lower Tier:

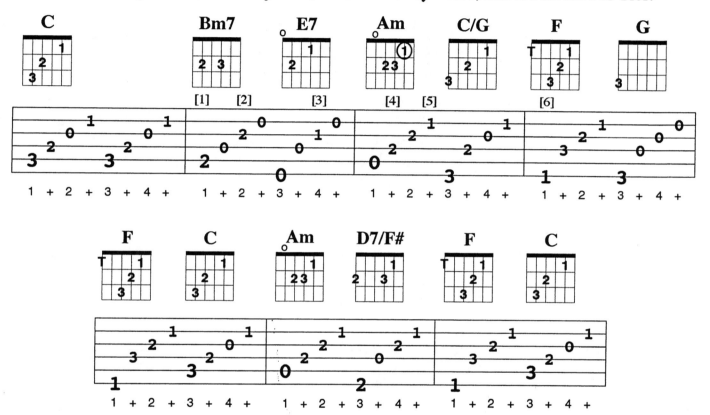

Several comments: This is the busiest example we've seen so far, where the chord changes come fast and furious and some of them involve complete refingerings. For example, after the C chord, the 2nd finger has to be Johnny-on-the-spot, moving immediately into position for the **Bm7** at [1]. But then the fingers responsible for the notes at [2], [3] and [4], can relax a bit, while still mindful of the boulder.

From [5] on, notice that ***the 1st finger spends a lot of time acting as an Anchor Finger*** at the 1st fret of the 2nd string (circled). More importantly, it's always the last note in the arpeggio, providing great cover for the removal and repositioning of fingers as needed and the covering up of *a lot* of pings. Every time you play that "1" in the Tab, some finger *other* than the 1st finger is moving into position for the next chord.

At [6], the Thumb comes first, then the rest of the **F** chord follows, probably all at once on Count 1+, as it did in "The Rose." And from **Am** to **D7/F#**, you can keep *both* the 1st and 3rd fingers as Anchors. Continuity, continuity, continu-

The examples that follow become increasingly "interesting."
If you find them *too* interesting, come back to them later. Here's
the Main Riff to Led Zeppelin's **"Babe, I'm Gonna Leave You:"**

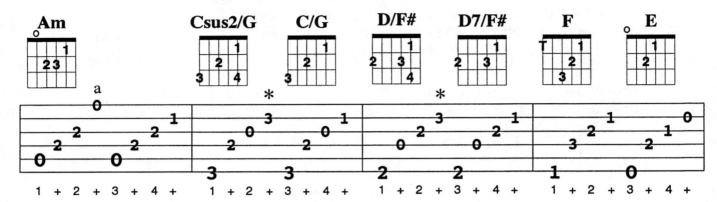

(1) Notes: We're not *exactly* introducing a new arpeggio in the 1st measure; **a** merely skips over the 2nd string (Lower Tier) in favor of 1st string and then returns home for the duration of the riff. (2) Except for the **F**, we let the last note of each arpeggio *ring over* into the next arpeggio. Happens to sound pretty good here. (3) The notes at the asterisks, played by the 4th finger, are added at the last moment. (4) The open 6th string in the **E** chord provides excellent cover for the *instantaneous* removal of the entire **F** chord.

(5) From the Chord Diagrams, you can see that *the 1st finger serves as an Anchor Finger* (C note on the 2nd string) all the way until the **E** chord. That's what accounts for the strange fingering for **D/F#**, which uses the unwieldy 4th finger. You add the **D/F#** notes one at a time as needed.

(6) The second time through, substitute the measure to the right for the 1st measure.

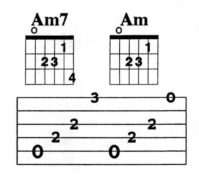

Next is the Main Riff from Weezer's **"The Sweater Song."** Yes, it's dissonant. Yes, Weezer.

Here we go up the neck, too, plunging us into the seedy underworld of **finger squeaks**. It is all too easy to produce these annoying little chirps on the wound bass strings, as we shift up and down the neck (at the asterisks).

It's just too tempting to leave our fingers in the chord shape, ease off the pressure a bit and just *slide* (the Guide Finger Principle). But that's where you get finger squeaks.

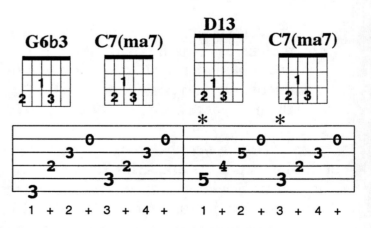

What to do? Well, you could let 'em squeak, if the sound doesn't bother you too much. (Obviously it bothers me or I wouldn't bring it up.) Or you could *briefly* lift off the strings altogether while your fingers are in transit, and there are two ways to do **that**. You could just leave early during the open 2nd string or wait until the last instant and *pounce*. Pouncing postpones the departure and keeps strings ringing a tad longer.

Now that we've done some position changing, let's do some more. Here's a chord progression that works for Dan Fogelberg's **"Longer,"** in the **Key of E**. We'll use partial chords.....because we can. And the 1st string is constantly ringing open, providing cover. For the two chords that move up the neck, I'll place a number on the right side of the diagram showing at which fret (4th and 6th frets here) the chord shape starts:

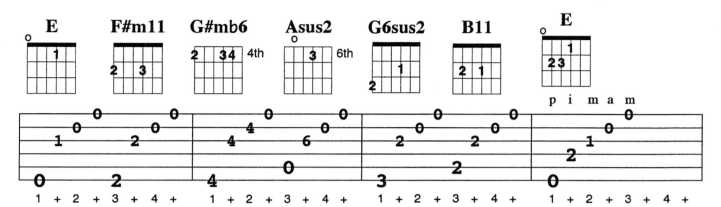

Well, we have similar issues in finger squeaking as we slide up the neck. But I would say that this time the squeaking isn't quite so heinous because you can do all the actual sliding on the *3rd* string, which doesn't squeak so badly because it's a thinner and more finely wound string. The 3rd finger appears in the 2nd, 3rd and 4th chords on the 3rd string, and contact can be maintained during this run. Just lift the 2nd finger off the big fat squeaky 6th string as you move. Then the 2nd finger Anchors and 1st finger Guides from **B11** to **E**.

Let's call all these nice open 1st-string notes we've been playing ***Escape Hatches****, since they allow the Fretting Hand to bail out early and reach the next chord in time.*

OKAY. Let's explore a **Worst-Case Continuity Scenario**.

Most of the time, when changing chords, you'll be able to use a currently unoccupied finger to get to the new note, or you'll have an Open String, an Escape Hatch, a Guide Finger, an Anchor Finger, *something*.

*But what if you **must** use the same finger twice in a row on different strings?* Here's a version of the "**Longer**" chord progression in the **Key of G** that has one huge opportunity to create one whopper of a discontinuity. I've marked the site. (If that **Bb6** stretch is too much, it won't really hurt to omit the 3rd finger.)

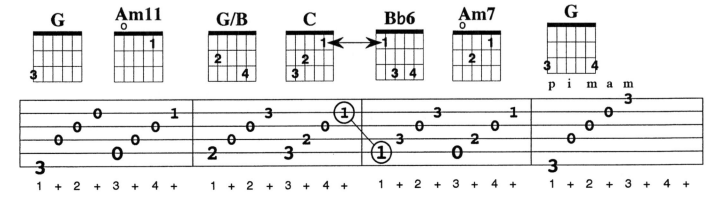

Christopher Parkening, fly fisherman and classical guitarist extraordinaire, once said (I'm paraphrasing) that, as ironic as it may seem, in order to get a smooth, continuous sound out of the guitar, your fingers must often move in sudden bursts of lightning speed.

This is what has to happen during that awkward transition. Your poor 1st finger must hang on until the bitter end of the **C** arpeggio and then appear *instantaneously* in the bass of the **Bb6** arpeggio, without so much as a how-do-you-do.

It's doable; think of it as target practice. I certainly wouldn't hurry the 3rd and 4th fingers into their respective positions in the **Bb6** until the 1st finger was settled on Count 1. But even if your aim is accurate, it can still sound a little ragged. Besides, being the dirty yellow dog that I am, I would prefer to avoid the whole situation. Here's a sneaky thing to do: ***Change the Picking Pattern!***

We'll call this *Arpeggio #2*. We aren't quite through using Arpeggio #1 yet, but we can certainly justify taking a look at something new. Actually, this is not a bad time to introduce some variety for the Picking Hand. It's probably best not to let any one pattern become *too* firmly entrenched. So here it is: Arpeggio #2 is a mutation of Arpeggio #1 where the order of the **m** and **a** fingers is reversed, so the finger sequence is now **p-i-a-m**. (And you can still omit the 3rd finger from the **Bb6**.) Play:

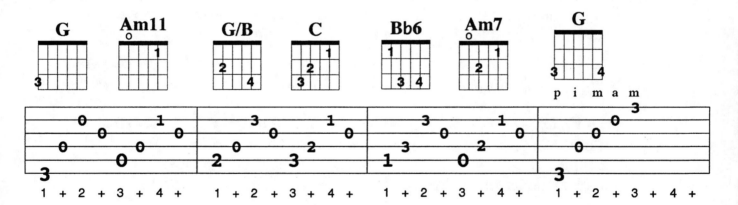

How was that? Feel a bit weird? Indeed, this pattern works out much better than the first pattern for this whole progression, since every chord in it contains an open 3rd string. With the **p-i-a-m** pattern, *we always play the 3rd string last, so it's always ringing open*. What a difference an Escape Hatch makes! The whole thing sounds a lot smoother now.

You know, there's no need to drop the *entire* **C** chord during the open-string diversion. You can keep the 2nd and 3rd fingers down a bit longer in the **C** chord while the 1st finger starts traveling (ping covered) to its next location. When the 1st finger arrives in the **Bb6**, it creates the next diversion and the two remaining fingers are finally freed and can move on to *their* new positions, just ahead of the boulder. It's all very cloak and dagger.

If you have some time to kill, take Arpeggio #2 and run through the chord progressions on page 8.....What's that? You've already done so on your own? I'm so proud!

Let's do one more exercise involving Arpeggio #1, something that will challenge the Fretting Hand a *lot* more without stressing the Picking Hand. In fact, the Picking Hand will play only the *first half* of each measure and then rest for the second half. These are the chords to a song titled "**Calling You**" from the film *Bagdad Cafe* (no "h" in this Bagdad), and I think it makes a nice little instrumental piece. ***But the chording is not simple.*** In other words, don't sweat this one.

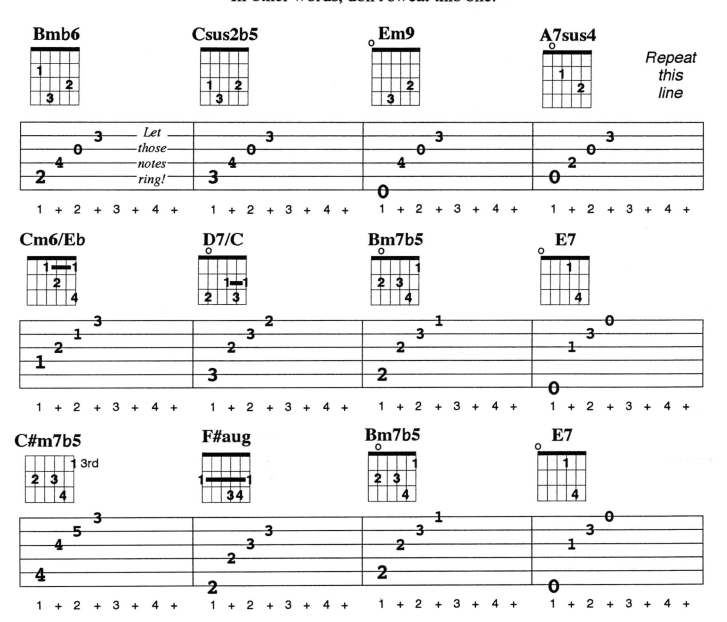

Haunting but hard. It helps to have that rest in every measure, giving the notes a chance to decay and softening the Ping Factor. But wait until the start of the next measure before making your move. In the 1st line, the 2nd finger remains as the Anchor and all the other fingers swirl around it. Then barre chords begin to show up (bring 'em on!).

To me, the hardest chord to get to is that first **Bm7b5**. This is another job for Indiana Jones, where each finger is added *just* as the boulder arrives. But from that point on, the 4th finger remains on the 2nd string in every chord, sometimes acting as an Anchor Finger and sometimes as a Guide Finger, and that's a great comfort.

A Brief Flirtation with Some Other Meters

The most common **meter**, or time structure, in Western Music is known as
4/4 Time (say "four-four"), and that's what we've been working with so far:
a situation where there are 4 strong beats (the numbered counts) in each
measure, with 4 weaker beats (the "+" counts) placed in between.
Let's take a break from 4/4 Time and try two other meters.

First, we visit the land of **3/4 Time**, where there is (take a guess) *one less*
beat per measure than in 4/4 Time. The simplest arpeggio in this meter starts off
with a 4-note Ascending Arpeggio, **p-i-m-a** (2 beats of music) and continues with
a Descending Arpeggio, **m-i** (1 more beat), giving the full sequence, **p-i-m-a-m-i**.
The notes on Counts 1, 2 and 3 are played a tad louder than those on the "+" counts.

Let's apply this *Arpeggio #3* to the same chords we saw in "**Longer**" in the **Key of G**.
*And be on the lookout for **another little trick** that helps us beat the boulder:*

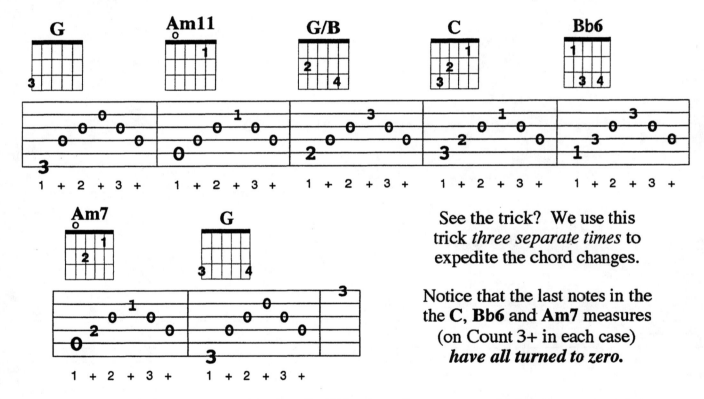

See the trick? We use this trick *three separate times* to expedite the chord changes.

Notice that the last notes in the the C, **Bb6** and **Am7** measures (on Count 3+ in each case) *have all turned to zero.*

We're releasing these 3 chords *a half beat early* so we can have some extra time
to make our chord changes. We have done this because we are lazy blighters who are
trying to get away with something. These open-string notes turn out to be *Artificial
Escape Hatches,* and as long as they give us a small advantage and don't
clash with the notes in the next chord, where's the harm?

In this example, the open D string sounds okay to me. Let your
own ear guide you. I'll say one thing: If you try this trick with
Arpeggio #1 between C and **Bb6** in "**Longer**," you'll have
an unpleasant aural experience. Try it. Blech:

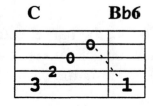

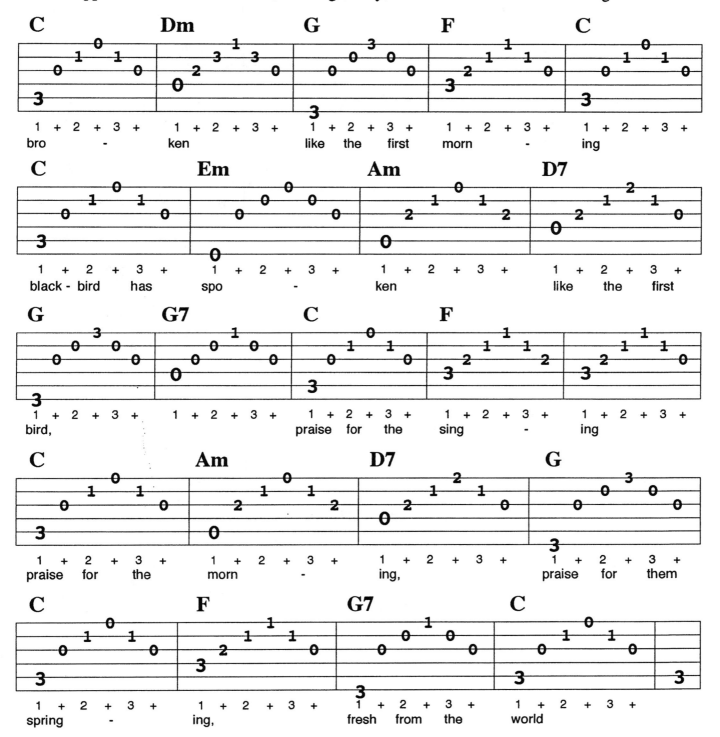

Next we'll do a song in **6/8 Time**, "House of the Rising Sun."
In *Guitar From Scratch*, I said that the meter of this song was 3/4 time.
Well, I was lying like a rug through my teeth, but I swear, it was for
your own good. I didn't want to confuse you with the facts.

Since the fraction 6/8 reduces to 3/4 anyway, how would the time signatures differ?
Well, it's purely a matter of how you distribute the *emphasis* across the measure.

Measures in both meters contain 6 little half-beats (still called Eighth Notes).
But in 3/4 Time, the grouping of the 6 notes is in *3 pairs;* that is, **1 + 2 + 3 +**,
whereas in 6/8 Time, the grouping is in *2 triplets,* to be counted **1 + a 2 + a**.
*So, 3/4 Time has 3 strong beats, each followed by one weak beat, and
6/8 Time has 2 strong beats, each followed by two weak beats.*

In **"House of the Rising Sun,"** the 1st and 4th notes in each measure (arrows)
are played a bit louder than the other notes. (In **"Morning Has Broken,"** it was
the 1st, 3rd and 5th notes that stood out.) We'll still call this Arpeggio #3,
since the finger sequence is the same; only the meter has changed:

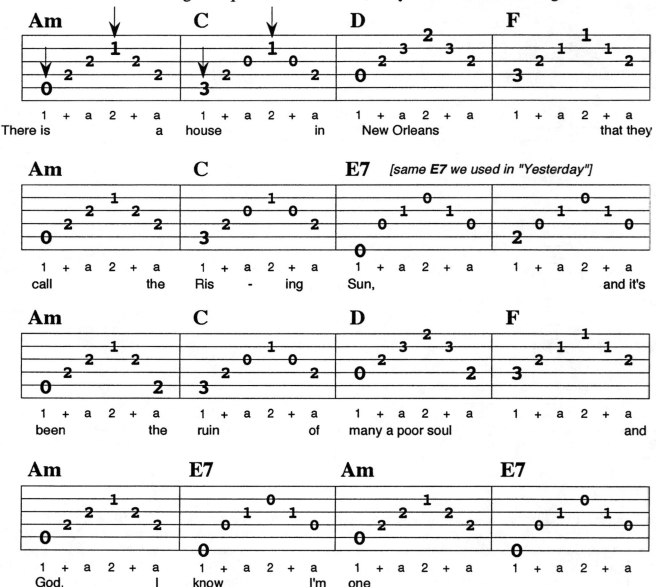

Did you see me get fancy in the 3rd line? I decided to throw in some **basslines**, devices that I introduced back in *Guitar From Scratch: The Sequel* that are designed to tie together the bass notes from one chord to the next. Instead of devoting all 6 notes in a measure to the arpeggio, we stop one note short and swap in a note that is intermediate to the bass notes that govern that measure and the next. Use the Thumb (**p**) for this.

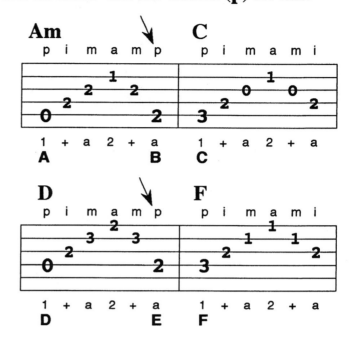

From **Am** to **C**, grab the B bass note on the 5th string (2nd finger, Count "a"), then the C bass of the **C** chord (3rd finger, Count 1). Then bring that 2nd finger back to the 4th string pronto to keep it ahead of the boulder. So we inject a little A-B-C bassline into the picking pattern.

From **D** to **F**, it's the 1st finger that does the bass line duty, because it's the closest. But as you move into **F**, the boulder starts a-rolling, and you lay the 3rd finger down first, followed immediately by the 2nd and then 1st finger. This is a D-E-F bass line.

I want to give you a little more practice playing in 3/4 Time versus 6/8 Time. Let's borrow a chord progression from the Intro to Emerson, Lake and Palmer's **"From the Beginning"** and play it in both meters, *being certain to emphasize the numbered counts*. (I've *enlarged* those notes in the Tab.)

This business happens way up the neck, starting at the 10th fret and ending at the 5th fret, with a 4th-string bass in the Higher Tier. Don't let the open 1st string throw off your ear. *Play each measure two times* and use the 2nd finger as the Guide Finger throughout. In the song, it's played in 3/4 Time, but I must say that 6/8 sounds pretty good, too:

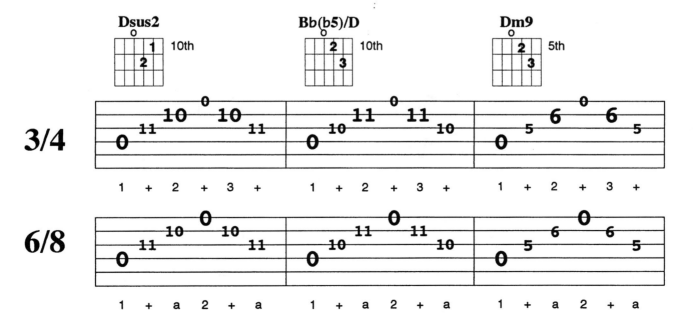

Slinking Back to 4/4 Time

"**Estudio**" (Spanish for "banana nut muffin." Or maybe "study") by Dionisio Aguado is a great way to introduce *Arpeggio #4*, a 3-finger pattern having the sequence: **p-i-m-i**. Here, **p** ranges from the 6th string all the way to the 3rd string, **i** is assigned to the 2nd string and **m** gets the 1st string, in an unusual sort of *High-High Tier*. And there's no **a** finger:

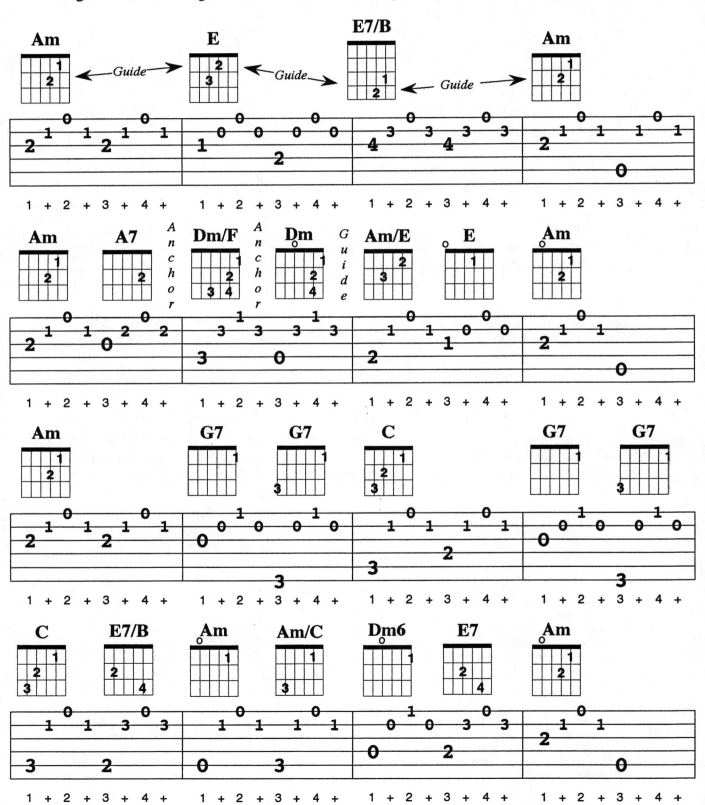

Some comments on **"Estudio"**: (1) It's supposed to be played *fast*. (Whenever.)

(2) In Line 1, that's an odd fingering for the **E** chord, but it gives us the opportunity to use *the 2nd finger as a Guide Finger for the entire line.* As you move the 2nd finger down from **Am** into **E**, there's no rush to put down the 3rd finger (4th string, 2nd fret) because you don't need it until Count 3. Then as you slide into the **E7/B**, the 1st finger returns.

(3) In the **Dm/F** chord in Line 2, you add the fretting fingers one at a time. Since it's not a common chord shape, you're better off not trying to land the whole thing at once; it's just too easy to flub a note or two and trigger a total cave in. Discretion is the better part of valor.

(4) You are wondering what's up with that funny **Am/E** chord. Left to our own devices, you and I would both choose to use the 1st and 2nd fingers, not the 2nd and 3rd. Believe it or not, 2-3 is the most efficient way to form this chord, especially if you retain the 2nd finger from way back in **A7** as indicated and use it to guide down to the 1st fret. But even better, this fingering is a set-up for the *next* chord, the one-finger **E**, where the 1st finger, having been denied participation in **Am/E**, is ready for action.

You could opt for the 1-2 fingering, but be forewarned: If you choose to use this more common fingering, you will come face to face with a Worst-Case Continuity Scenario, where the 1st finger is responsible for both the *last* note in the **Am/E** arpeggio and the *first* note in the very next **E** arpeggio. Go-go-go.

(5) Arpeggio #4 is a rather skimpy creature; our previous patterns have sported 4 different notes, but this one only has 3. That's kind of a bare minimum if you want to be able to identify a chord quality. Even with 3, you still might not be able to distinguish a Major chord from a Minor chord.

Try Arpeggio #4 on the sort of chord progression that shows up in the Beatles' **"Blackbird."** (It won't sound *exactly* like "Blackbird.") The 4th finger is the Guide Finger. Pretty, no?

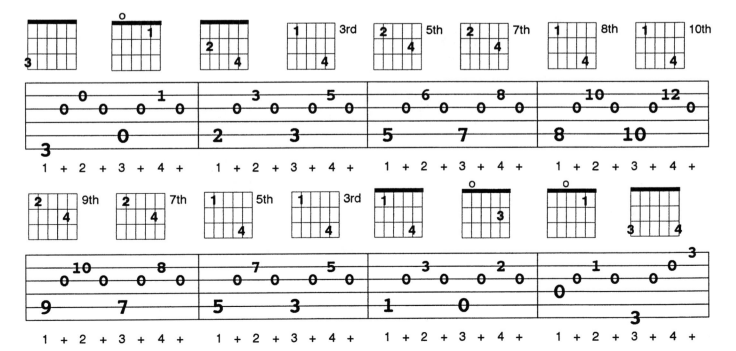

Feel the need to try something completely different? Check out the Travis-Style section (page 44).

Meet the Twins

So Arpeggio #4 sounded kind of scrawny, with its 3 measly notes.
One way to fatten it up would be to **twin** the **a** finger with the **m** finger.
Behold *Arpeggio #5:* **p - i - ma - i**. Try it with the chords to "**Yesterday**":

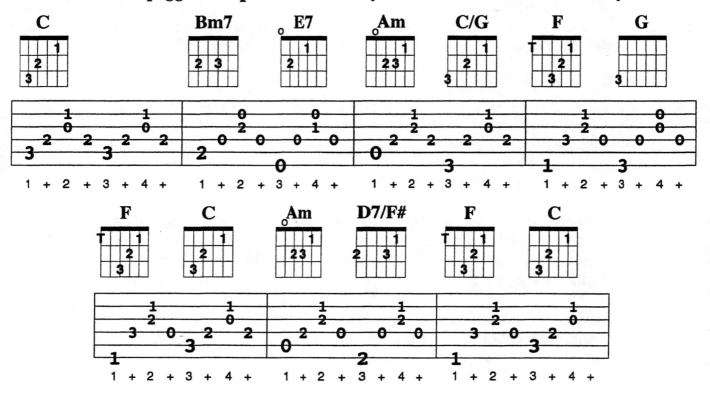

I like to keep the tips of the twinned fingers pressed together a little so that they move as a unit. You need to make sure that the attack is balanced so that one finger doesn't overpower the other. It helps if the nails are the same length.

I also threw in 4 Artificial Escape Hatches: between (1) **F** and **G**, (2) **F** and **C**, (3) **Am** and **D7/F#** and (4) **F** and **C** again. Sometimes you just want to take it easy. I could have put one between **C** and **Bm7**, but my ear told me that that one might be one step over the line. Of course, you might feel that the ones I *did* put in sounded a little cheesy. Me, I think I'll be able to sleep tonight.

Here is the 1st line of "**The Rose**" similarly duded up:

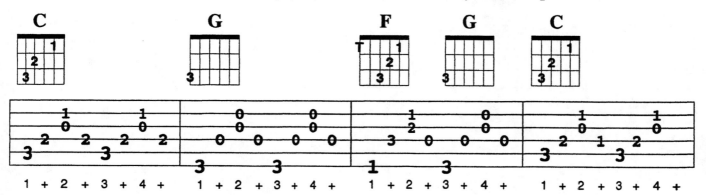

Some Other Simple Arpeggios

It seems only fair that we play a *De*scending Arpeggio for a change, and we'll call it *Arpeggio #6*. For some reason these just aren't as common.

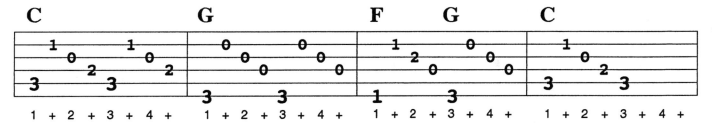

I haven't said it in a while, so forgive me if I explicitly reiterate a key principle: **Keep adjacent fingers assigned to adjacent strings.** If you learn nothing else.....

It's time to introduce a fingerstyle technique known as the **pinch**, where the Thumb, moving downward, plays at *exactly the same time* as one or more of the fingers, moving upward, resulting in a pinching motion. The simplest approach is to play **p** and **m** together, followed by **i**. This is how those chords from **"Blackbird"** are really supposed to be played. A pleasant, balanced tension exists between **p** and **m** just before the strings are released. Here are those chords again; I've spread out the Tab numbers to make room for the chord diagrams. This is *Arpeggio #7*.

It's back to 4-finger arpeggios for the next two examples. The first one, *Arpeggio #8*, starts with a pinch between **p** and **a** and moves into a Descending Arpeggio. The second one, *Arpeggio #9*, starts with the same pinch but then proceeds with an Ascending Arpeggio:

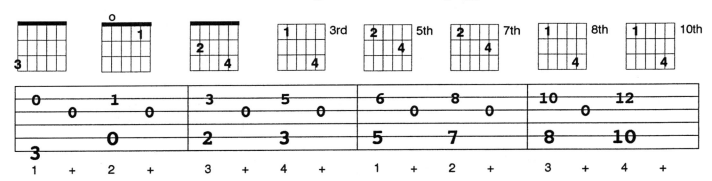

Let's move to the Higher Tier and light the fuse on **"Pachelbel's Canon."**
The 6th-string bass from the **Em** chord may, unfortunately, ring over into the **F** chord,
causing a dissonance. See if you can stop it from vibrating with your left thumb as
you begin the **F**. We'll start with Arpeggio #1, just to whet your appetite:

A pinch variation on Arpeggio #9, *Arpeggio #10* uses **a** to both start and finish each chord:

Arepggio #11 simply takes Arpeggio #10 and twins **a** with **m** in the pinch:

Arpeggio #12 staggers around a bit, and each chord both starts and ends with **m**:

In *Arpeggio #13*, it is **i** and **m** that are twinned instead of **m** and **a**, and there is no pinch:

Arpeggios with Longer Sequences

So far, our arpeggios have run to the short side, each one occupying half a measure at most. Now we'll look at some non-repeating sequences that *last an entire measure*. It doesn't matter if you know these songs or not; just use the chords to go exploring.

Arpeggio #14 is from Eric Clapton's **"Wonderful Tonight."** The sequence is **p-i-m-i-a-m-i-m**:

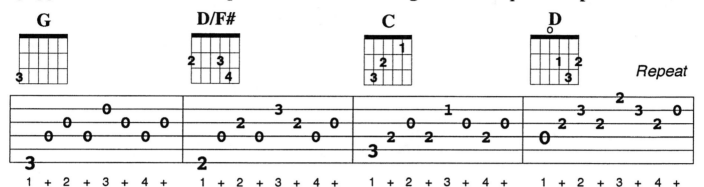

I love that riff; it has so much variety packed into such a small space, making use of all three basses and both tiers. There's that awkward **D/F#** again; you certainly could refinger it without the 4th finger, but then there would be extra movement to switch to **C**. You might as well put that 4th finger to work beyond just the standard **G** and **B7** chords. And don't miss the Artificial Escape Hatches from **D/F#** to **C** and from **D** back to **G**.

"December," by Collective Soul, uses *Arpeggio #15*, **p-i-m-i-m-a-m-i**, and a bassline:

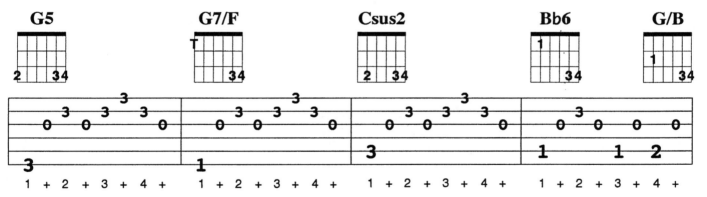

And *Arpeggio #16*, from **"The Freshmen,"** by the Verve Pipe, uses yet another slightly different sequence of fingers, **p-i-m-i-a-i-m-i**, both tiers, three basses and a bassline:

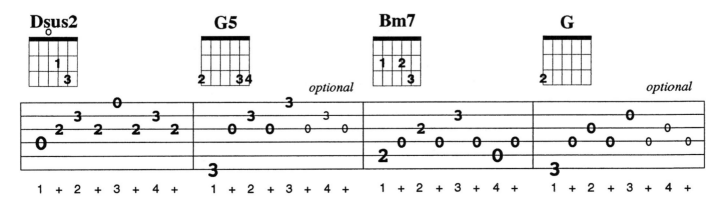

Here's an instrumental passage from Pink Floyd that asks the musical question, **"Is There Anybody Out There?"** *Arpeggio #17*, with the sequence **p-i-m-a-m-i-p-i**, starts things off. Notice the possible alternate fingering for the **Am** chord:

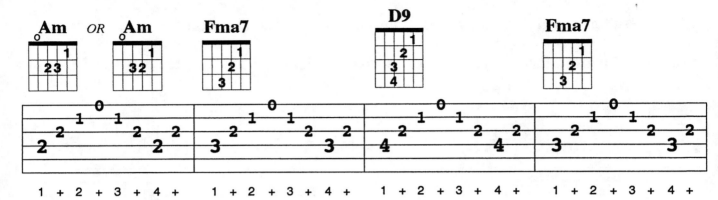

Arpeggio #17 is no more than Arpeggio #3, from 3/4 Time, plus two more notes thrown in at the end to lengthen it to 4/4 Time.

Do you see why it might be nice to use the second fingering for **Am**? All you need to do to get to **F** is to scoot the 3rd finger up one fret. Personally, I'd stick with the normal **Am** and just deal with this Worst-Case Continuity Scenario for the 3rd finger. I kinda *like* the normal **Am** and I don't mind the rapid transition. You can overdo being ready.

For **D9**, I would try to hang on to the **Fma7** shape, partly because it seems to be easier to press down all 4 fingers in a stretch like that, and partly because we're going back to the **Fma7** immediately thereafter. This time, I would say that we are *not* overdoing being ready, but that's just my own judgement call.

Now for the 2nd line:

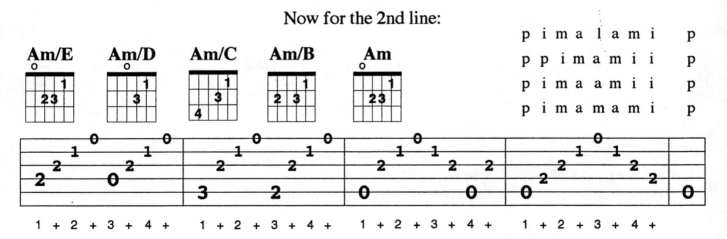

Looks like we're back to Arpeggio #1 for the first two measures, albeit with a bassline that runs down the scale (E-D-C-B-A). The 3rd measure is Arpeggio #17 again, and then the last measure, *Arpeggio #18*, deserves some comment. We've come up against this situation before, where we need to play notes on 5 different strings using only 4 fingers.

Above the 4th measure you see a number of alternatives, the most obvious being to ignore classical dogma (!!!) and trot out the 4th finger of the Fretting Hand ("l" for little) to grab that 5th note. Otherwise, we change tiers and use some fingers twice in a row.

Let's return both to the classical world and to Arpeggio #16
with Mauro Giuliani's smash fingerstyle hit, "**Allegro**":

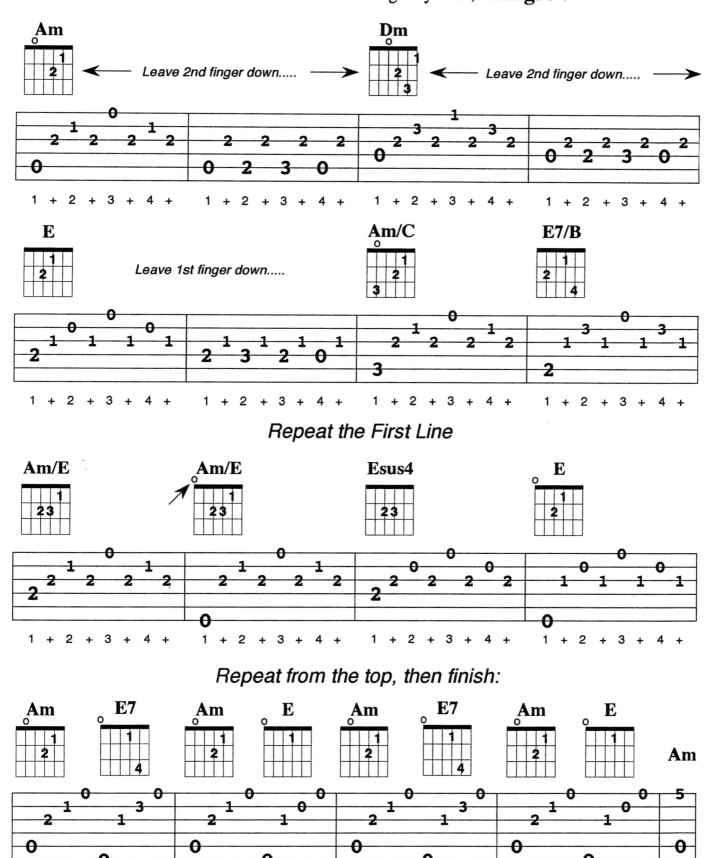

Comments on "Allegro":

(1) I've mentioned before how classical players tend to hold down only the notes that they plan to play. In the 1st line, this fingering of **Am** is an expression not only of economy within the chord itself but also of *continuity* throughout the rest of the line, *since the 2nd finger remains as an Anchor*. In the 2nd measure, the 2nd finger stays put during that bass line, as the 1st finger plays the bass B note and the 3rd finger plays the following C note. Then **Dm** benefits from the continued presence of the 2nd finger in the 3rd and 4th measures. Hang on!

(2) Then, naturally, after all that aid and comfort, you have a Worst-Case Scenario for the 2nd finger from **Dm** to **E**, and an Artificial Escape Hatch won't help (bad sound). Well, sometimes that's how the cookie bounces and you're just caught in a yank. Then **Am/C** is okay, but then comes another yank on the way to the **E7/B**.

(3) The 4th line is a breeze, and this time you do need to finger the entire **Am** chord.

(4) The last line is Arpeggio #1 all the way. Notice that each chord starts and stops with an open string, meaning that you have at least 2 open strings in a row between refingerings. So the question is: How much of this slack time should we take advantage of?

Answer: only about half of it. Hang on to the chord through the ringing of the open 1st string, ignoring the Escape Hatch, and then make your move *under the cover of the open bass string that starts the next arpeggio*. If you do this, you'll allow the *fretted* notes of each arpeggio to ring a bit longer and still have plenty of time to refinger during the open bass note.

- -

I want to show you another full-measure pattern, *Arpeggio #19*, but this one's a bit squirrelly. It's related to an Afro-Cuban rhythm known as **clave**. An unusual grouping of the 8 notes is what will take some getting used to. Normally, in a measure of 4/4 Time, we have 4 pairs of Eighth notes, or **duplets**, where the first note (on the numbered count) gets more emphasis than the second note (on the "+" count).

But this rhythm is based more on the *triplet* rather than the duplet, as in 6/8 Time. Of course, in 6/8 Time, you have 6 slots in the measure, room for exactly 2 triplets. Can you see what's going to be the problem with this rhythm? There are 8 slots to fill, and the number 3 doesn't go into the number 8 evenly. So we need *two triplets plus one duplet*, yielding 3 + 3 + 2 = 8. Let's call it **3/3/2**.

Hold down an **Am** chord and play the finger sequence **p-i-m-p-i-m-p-i**. It has a lop-sided sound. To the right, the first measure keeps the same bass note and the second measure uses different bass notes.

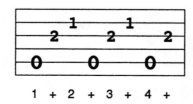 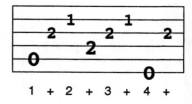

The unsettling part about **3/3/2** comes at the end of the measure, after you've played the two triplets, and what you *really* want to do is *play another triplet*. But no. You must cut off that triplet in its prime and convert it into a duplet. Here's Gregg Allman's **"Multi-Colored Lady."** We use the High-High Tier again, with **p** in charge of 4 strings:

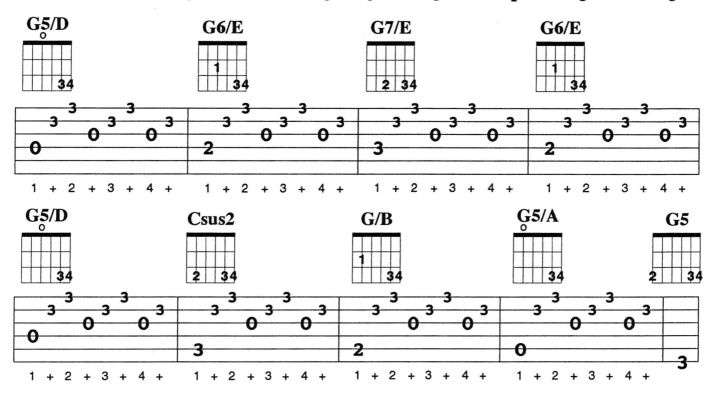

The **3/3/2** rhythm is more versatile when you twin **m** with **a** *(Arpeggio #20)*. Here are the 1st lines of my arrangements of Roy Orbison's **"Blue Bayou"** and Jim Croce's **"I'll Have to Say I Love You in a Song."**

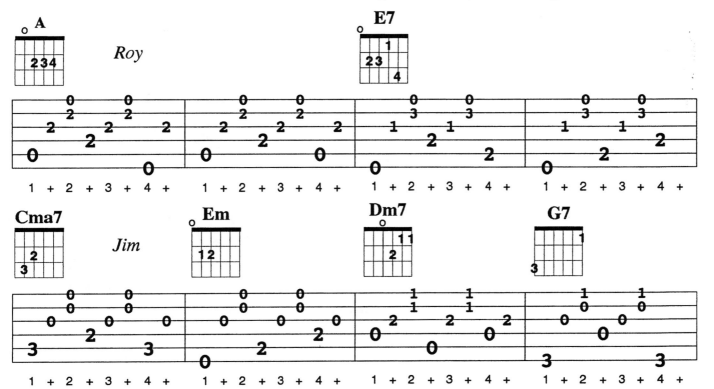

Twenty Arpeggios: A Retrospective

Seems like a good time to have a little recap. The twenty arpeggios we've seen so far are merely a good starting point. I should stress the fact that the possible variations are endless. And while we'll spend the rest of this section fooling around with many of these variations, I wouldn't blame you if you stopped right here and started drilling these arpeggios in as many songs as possible. Then when you got good and bored, you could move on.

p = Thumb   *i* = Index finger   *m* = Middle finger   *a* = Ring finger

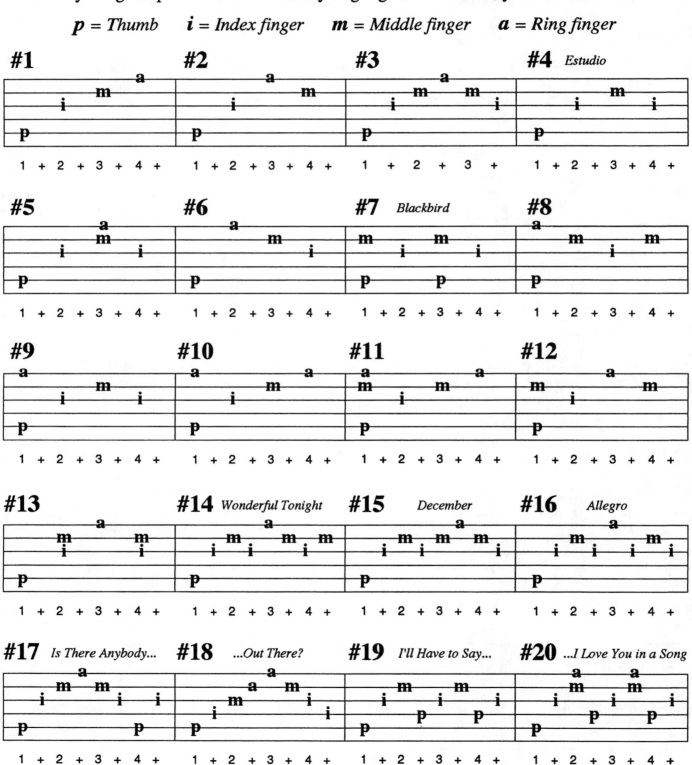

Again, feel free to look ahead at the simpler Travis-Style stuff starting on page 44.

Mixing Quarter Notes and Eighth Notes

Up to this point, we've been avoiding playing notes with different time values in the same measure. Any of our patterns could have been played either as Eighth Notes, eight "quick" beats to the measure, or Quarter Notes, four "slow" beats to the same measure. A four-note arpeggio played using Quarter Notes would fill up an entire measure in 4/4 Time, but if you played those notes as Eighth Notes, you could fit two arpeggios into the same measure.

Four Quarter Notes

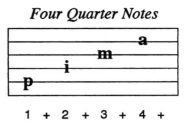

Eight Eighth Notes

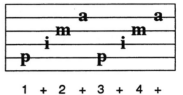

Well, there's no reason why we can't mix the two types of notes in the same measure of music. But there's a problem: *A lot of people have a hard time keeping the rhythm.*

Clearly, I'm not directing this comment toward you. I'm sure *your* rhythm is as reliable as an atomic clock. No, I'm talking to the three or four other people who have bought this book. So you can just skip ahead a bit.

Actually, everybody seems to have at least some trouble with this. Part of your brain needs to keep track of the **underlying pulse** of the piece: **1** + 2 + 3 + 4 + **1** + 2 + 3 + 4 +, because you *won't always* be playing a note on every one of those little beats. Here are some examples; mind the gaps:

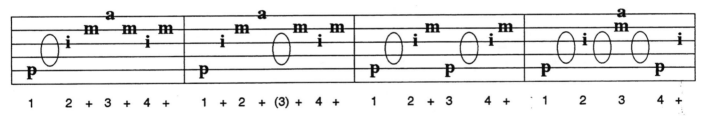

The best thing you can do when you're working on a measure with mixed note values is to firmly count aloud, "One-and-Two-and-Three-and-Four-and." A metronome might help, but if you're like me, you'll become so absorbed that you'll start ignoring it. Everyone has a natural sense of rhythm (you have a heartbeat, I assume). Surrender to The Force. Wild animals can smell fear and they can tell when you drop a beat.

Some random examples of riffs that have gaps in them: **"Kryptonite,"** by 3 Doors Down (2 Escape Hatches and a Low-Low Tier), and **"Coconut,"** by Nilsson (changing bass).

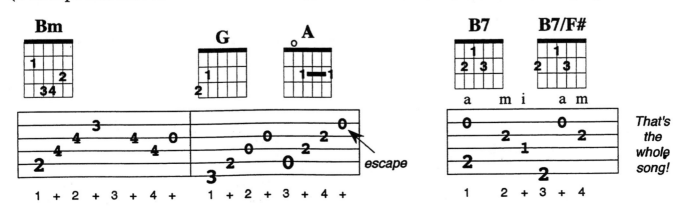

Meet the Trio

I'll bet you've been waiting for the other shoe to drop. If we can *twin* fingers together to play two notes at once, why can't we *triple* them to play three? But what to call them? The Triplets? Already spoken for in musical jargon. The Triad? Same problem. The Trinity? Too majestic. The Three Stooges? Too close for comfort. Let's go with the **Trio**.

If you take the Trio and pair it with the Thumb, you have what I call a Grand Pinch. In a way, playing a Grand Pinch at the start of a measure is like showing everybody your hand at the beginning of a card game or fast-forwarding to the end of the video: The mystery is gone. Then again, there is certainly no doubt about the harmonic identity of the chord you are playing. For instance, if you play a **Dm** chord with Arpeggio #1, you don't find out that it has a Minor chord quality until you get to the *4th note*. Could have been **D** Major up to that point.

Here are several ways that the Trio can be incorporated into arpeggios (G chord):

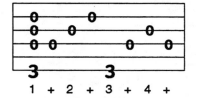 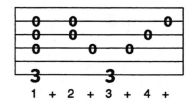 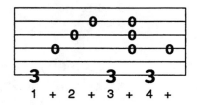

In "Tears in Heaven," Eric Clapton plays a pattern that uses both a Trio and a Grand Pinch. Here is a chord sequence taken from the Bridge Section:

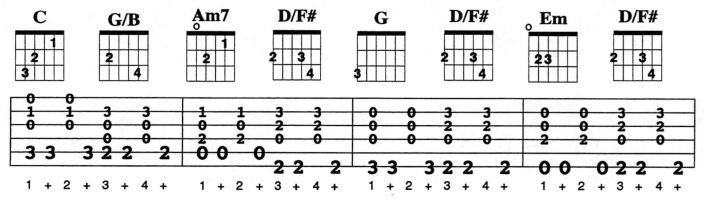

Some of those chord changes need to come almost instantaneously, since each pattern starts and finishes with the bass note. Feel free to experiment with different fingerings for the **D/F#**. But where the Trio and the Grand Pinch really come in handy is when the chords change *on every beat* and you have no time to casually deal out a pretty arpeggio. *You must go now!* (Technically, these things don't qualify as arpeggios because they aren't "broken" chords.)

Situations like this don't arise too often. (Good, right?). There's no wiggle room here. You may feel the boulder gently brushing the nape of your neck, but you can beat it, Indy.

More Samples From the Field

I thought we'd wrap up this section of the book with some more examples of arpeggios from popular music. Some of them are unique to only one song, but you'll get an idea of just how far we Fingerstyle Guitarists can go with 10 fingers, 6 strings and almost one brain.

On the left is "**My Friends,**" by the Red Hot Chili Peppers, using the Twins to great advantage and changing tiers, and on the right is "**I'm Sensitive,**" by Jewel. Me too.

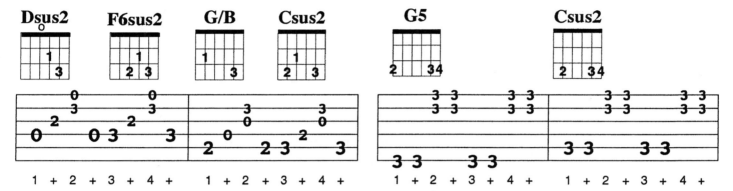

Here's the Intro to Bon Jovi's "**Wanted Dead or Alive.**" This is a good workout for the Picking Hand because **m** is completely excluded, and it hates that. There are two chord shapes moving down the neck and the 2nd finger acts as the Guide Finger:

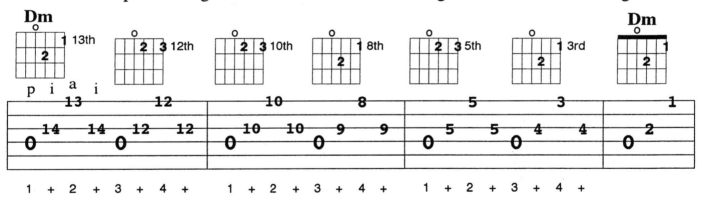

From Metallica's *only* love song, "Nothing Else Matters," here's an accompaniment part from the Verse. Two variations on the same chords and mixed note values in 3/4 Time:

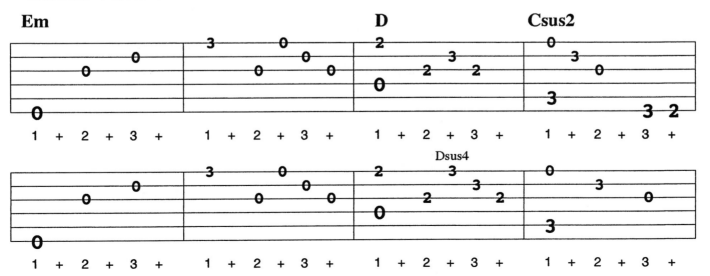

By now, I hope that the fingers of the Picking Hand have resolved any power struggles and that each finger is doing its own job at its own station without complaint. I hope that no one is eating anyone else's lunch. You shall not side with the great against the powerless.

As to the Fretting Hand, it's time to play *Silent Running*, and welcome to today's show. Our contestant (guess who) will be competing with him- or herself for the self-satisfaction of being able to move chord forms up and down the guitar neck with perfect composure and without so much as a *whisper* due to sloppy finger movements. Our category is *Paul Simon's Guitar Part in "Scarborough Fair."* Here comes the Main Riff:

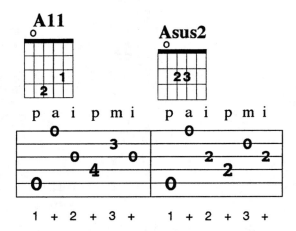

Round One. Get the Picking Hand going by playing multiple reps on one chord at a time, over and over. It's an odd little pattern in 3/4 Time, Higher Tier, **p** alternating between 5th- and 4th- string basses. What's irritating is that **m** *wants to jump in and play something right away*, as it ever does, but it is forced to wait until near the end of the pattern. What an ego.

Round Two. Once you get a good roll going with one chord, shift back and forth between the two chords using the 2nd finger as a Guide Finger. This two-measure, repeating phrase constitutes about half the song.

Round Three. Notice two things. First, you're squeaking like a cat toy. Unless you have flatwound strings or some gunk on your fingers, you're going to wake the neighbors. Second, *more than half the notes you're playing are on open strings and most of them come **between** the two chords*.

This is where several lightbulbs should be going on in your head. Not only is there no rush to switch chords, but there is also enough time to *completely remove* your fingers from the strings during transit, circumventing any public squeaking engagements.

Start with the **A11** chord. At the end of the 1st measure, lift your fingers but ***keep playing the arpeggio***. You've got *2 entire open strings* at the start of the 2nd measure (gobs of time) during which you can shift your hand down the 2 frets and form your fingers into a *floating* **Asus2** shape. Then on Count 2, just in the nick of time, you deftly set down the chord.

Now you're playing the **Asus2** in the 2nd measure. Upon returning to the 1st measure, you notice, with glee, that this time there are *3 entire open strings* before the next fretted note, almost enough time to take on a second job, at least in fingerstyle guitar terms. Now you're beginning to feel jaunty, perhaps a bit smug, as you calmly tool back and forth between the chords without even a peep of extraneous string noise.

But you need to ***keep the Picking Hand going*** between chord placements. This must be the perfect exercise for creating independence between the Fretting and Picking Hands.

Do we have a special parting gift for our contestant? You bet we do! Here's the rest of **"Scarborough Fair."** To save space, I'll just put the words "Main Riff" whenever you're supposed to play it.

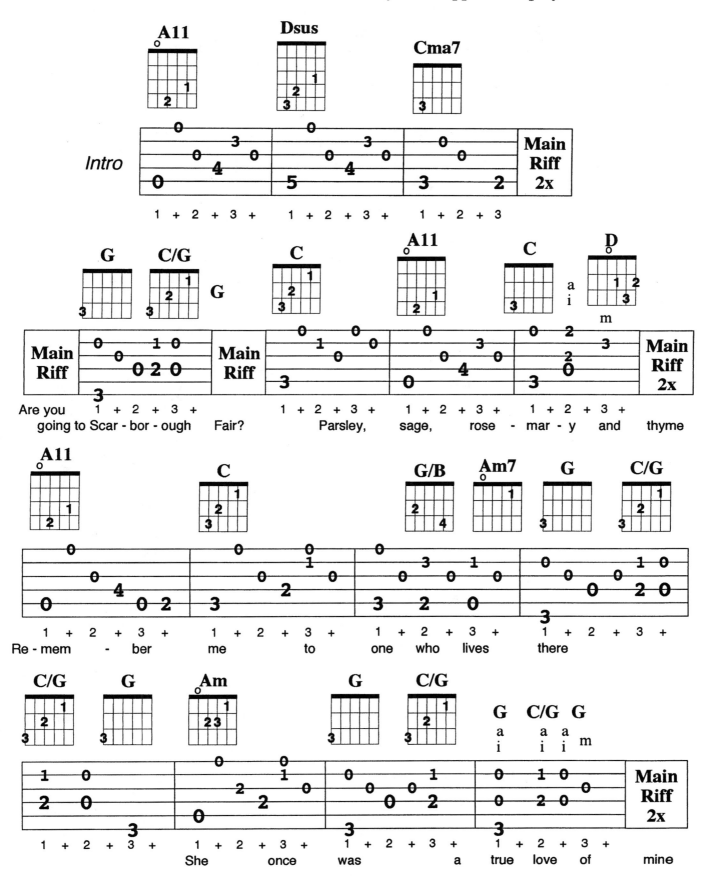

The Verse to Jim Croce's **"Time in a Bottle"** uses Arpeggio #3 on the Higher Tier, so the Picking Hand has it easy (until special **intervals**, called **6ths**, take us up the neck.) The Fretting Hand will be more of a challenge due to several rather serious stretches.

The 3rd finger is the Anchor Finger for the 1st line.
The 4th finger does some anchoring as well:

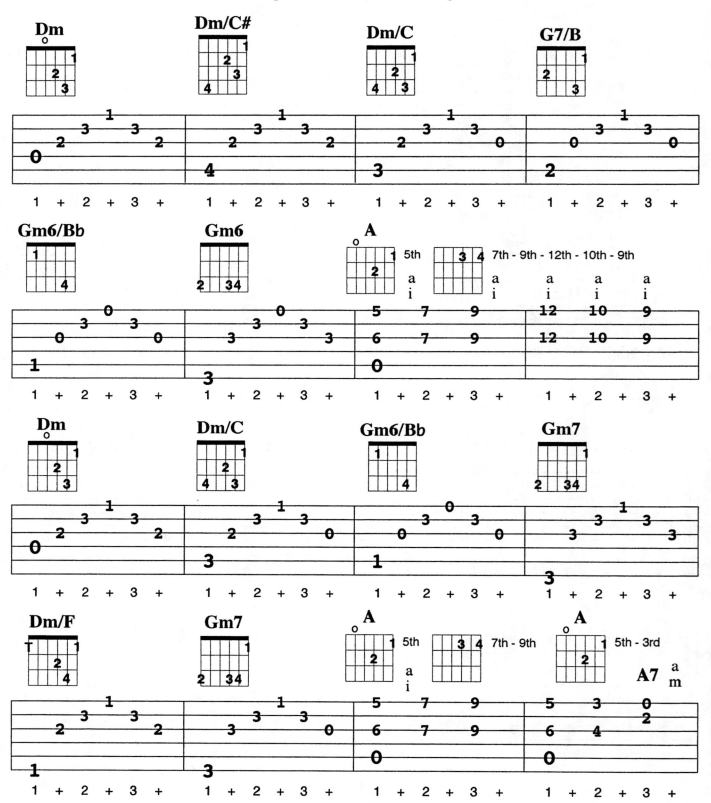

And here's the Chorus to **"Time in a Bottle"** (play it twice). This arpeggio is what happens when you take Arpeggio #5 and adapt it to 3/4 Time: **p-i-ma-i-ma-i**. Yep, it's the Twins. And this time, the boulder is bearing down particularly hard during the barre chord transitions. Well, **D** to **F#m/C#** isn't so bad (move the 3rd finger first, then lay the barre down), but you really need to hustle to extend that barre to the 5th string for the **Bm7** (where the 3rd finger becomes an Anchor Finger into **D/A**):

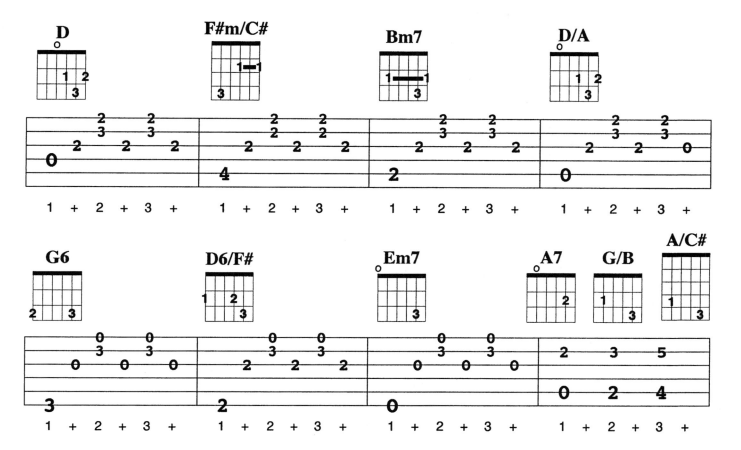

Where's James Taylor?

Don't even get me started. There is enough fingerstyle material there to fill a book (another project). And while it's not extremely difficult, neither is it particularly easy. To give you at least a taste, here's one version of the Intro to **"Carolina in My Mind."** It's all Higher Tier and mostly Quarter Notes; watch the timing of the Eighth Notes:

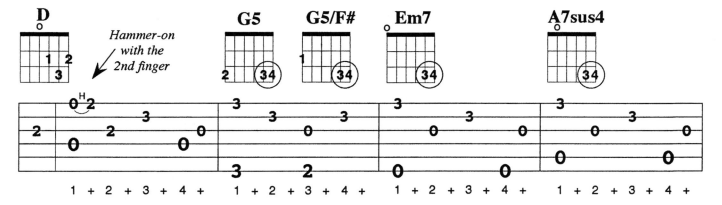

Finally, let's take a trip to Brazil and look at the basic **Bossa Nova** guitar riff. We use the Thumb and the Trio again, but interestingly, the two units come together in a Grand Pinch *only once* in the entire two-measure pattern (in the middle). The Thumb always comes on Counts 1 and 3, while the Trio comes 3 times on the beat and 4 times between beats ("+" counts). You just have to learn the pattern by rote, I'm afraid. Try it with a **G** chord and ***count it out:***

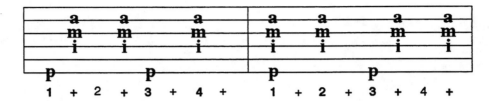

So that wasn't so easy, was it? Well, it gets worse with the jazz chords. Here's the first half of the Verse to "**Girl From Ipanema.**" Chords can change in mid-pattern!

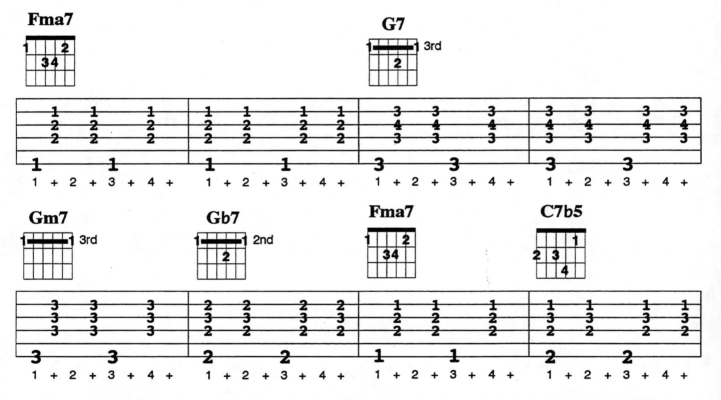

Repeat all of the above, keeping the last **Fma7** for both measures, omitting the **C7b5**. You can do this with an Alternating Bass (below), but you must modify the chords (belower):

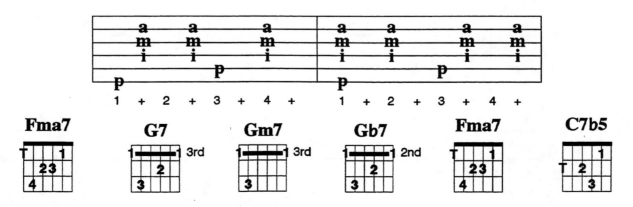

Here are the chords to the Bridge for **"Girl From Ipanema."** The Ninth chords have a fairly easy Alternating Bass, so I've written it out that way. Those **X**'s you see represent the deadened strings that you'll inevitably create as you change positions during the chord changes. Just keep your fingers resting lightly on the strings as you travel between chords and you'll mute them out nicely:

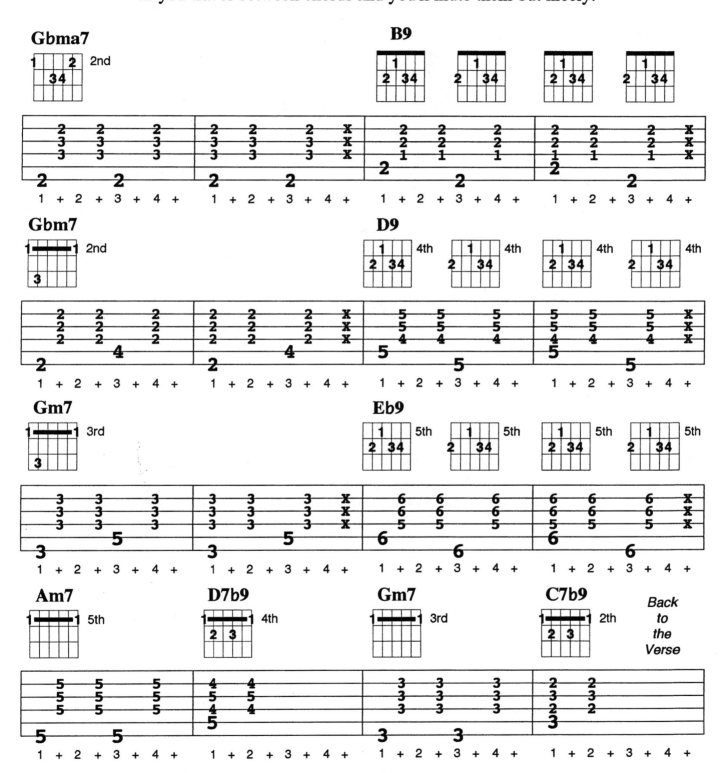

I probably shouldn't have shown you that; perhaps once the pain and confusion subside, you'll find a way to forgive me. But some readers might already be more accomplished with the Fretting Hand and would enjoy taking on such a challenge.

Part Two: Travis-Style Basics

Travis-Style fingerpicking, or **Travis-Picking**, is a fingerstyle sub-genre. It's named after Merle Travis, who learned it from Mose Rager and Ike Everly (father of the Everly Brothers), who in turn had picked it up from the black musical traditions of eastern Kentucky, where they all lived. Many black musicians, including Mississippi John Hurt, Reverend Gary Davis and Blind Blake, played this piedmont blues style, and one could argue that it should be named after one of them. But Travis was the one who brought it into popular music, so he gets the nod.

The term "Travis-Picking" has become shorthand for any kind of an **Alternating Bass** picking pattern. The role of the Thumb is to keep a steady beat going between two or three bass strings while the fingers do "something else" on the treble strings. That something else can be either (1) part of a *repeated pattern* that feels connected to the Thumb's motion or (2) an *independent melody line* that relies on the Thumb just to keep steady time. We'll focus on the repeated pattern, which is the easier of the two and does lead to the melody approach.

Technically, a Travis-Picking pattern is an arpeggio (a broken chord), but it seems to be more than that, as the alternating bassline takes on a function of its own. Compared to the playing we've done so far, you'll feel as if Travis-Picking *overuses* the Thumb. Before, the Thumb was just another finger that happened to be assigned to the bassline. Now it's responsible for hammering out the rhythm too, specifically a "Boom-Chick" (or "Tick-Tock" or "Oom-Pah") rhythm.

To someone exposed to Travis-Picking for the first time, it seems almost like sleight of hand. You see it happening and you hear it, but you don't get it. The first time I saw it happening, I couldn't figure out what was going on, and I had studied classical guitar and thought I'd seen it all! *It sounds like two guitars are playing*. Chet Atkins kept getting fired from his radio jobs in the '40s and '50s because he sounded like two mediocre guitar players. Guess he did better on TV where they could *see* him.

Okay. Hold down a **C** chord if you're optimistic about learning to Travis-Pick, and hold down an **Am** chord if you're pessimistic. (That was a veiled reference to the fact that Major chords sound "Happy" and Minor chords sound "Saddish.") Both of these chords have Root Notes, C and A, on the 5th string, and we will normally want to hear these stable, grounded notes first in any Travis-Picking pattern, as we do in all arpeggio playing.

So. Play the 5th string with your Thumb (*boom*) and then the 4th string with your very same Thumb (*chick*). Do this a number of times, keeping a *steady* count of **1 - 2 - 3 - 4** (*boom-chick-boom-chick*). That's 2 boom-chicks per measure. These are downward strokes of the Thumb, the whole Thumb and *nothing but the Thumb*. Don't sneak the Index Finger in there. *It's all about the Thumb!*

Let's see the Tab for this, with one
measure, or two cycles of alternation.
Play it *ad nauseum infinitum:*

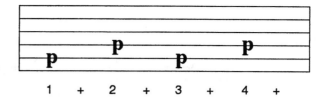

This may not seem like such a big deal, but this little maneuver is to Travis-Picking what carbon is to life on earth---pretty darned useful, I'd say. It's like the ape in apricot. Much of what we do for the rest of this book will depend on this alternating bassline. Sure, it's easy to play right now, but we'll start adding layers of complexity that will make it harder and harder to hang on to this strictly alternating bass. But hang on you must.

Now that we've dug the hole and laid the foundation, it's time to do some framing. As you know, in one measure of 4/4 Time, there is enough room for 4 Quarter Notes, 8 Eighth Notes or some combination of the two that adds to **One**. In Travis-Picking, *the bass notes are Quarter Notes that **must live on the beat** (Counts 1, 2, 3 and 4). The treble notes played by the fingers can live anywhere in the measure, either on the beat (1-2-3-4) or between beats (the "+" counts).*

Now, there's no need to fill up all eight slots with notes, but for the first pattern, this is exactly what we'll do. *It's actually harder to leave notes out.* Bass notes will occupy the four numbered counts and treble notes will occupy the four "+" counts.

First let's create the shortest non-repeating sequence possible, the half measure, by inserting some treble note after the bass notes. Hold down **C** or **Am** and play:

(1) The 5th string with **p**
(2) The 3rd string with **i**
(3) The 4th string with **p**
(4) The 2nd string with **m**

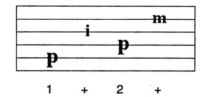

Play that sequence twice in a row so
that it fills an entire measure and you
have a pattern we'll call *Travis #1:*

Play the Travis #1 pattern 98.6 times.

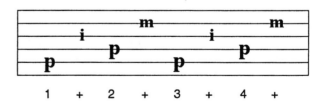

Already you'll be astounding those friends of yours who swore you'd never amount to a thing. I like to call this a **5/4** pattern because the Thumb alternates between the 5th and 4th strings. But before you get too comfortable, there is also a **6/4** version of Travis #1, since there are chords like **G** and **Em** that have their Root Notes on the 6th string. Behold:

Play **G** or **Em** a buncha times. I would
still like to call it Travis #1, since everything
stays just the same except for the Root Note.
It may feel a bit funny skipping over that
5th string, but you'll learn to love it.

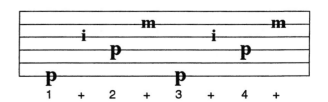

Comments:

(1) Chet Atkins said that when he was first able to get that Thumb to go back and forth, that's all he did for the next 15 years (oh sure; more like 15 *minutes*), but he was making an important point: The Thumb is the critical factor here. We "overuse" the Thumb because it drives the pattern. It's like the engine room of a battleship, just churning away, supplying the power for moving forward. Just because we've added the fingers doesn't mean we can let up on the Thumb. Focus on the Thumb!

(2) Be sure, once you do add the fingers, that *the Thumb keeps moving at the same speed.* Try these exercises for the **5/4** and **6/4** basses to get the Thumb and fingers in sync. If the speed you choose for the Thumb is too fast to accommodate the fingers, slow the whole thing down. *Speed is not your friend. If you can't play it slow, you can't play it fast.* **Be smooth:**

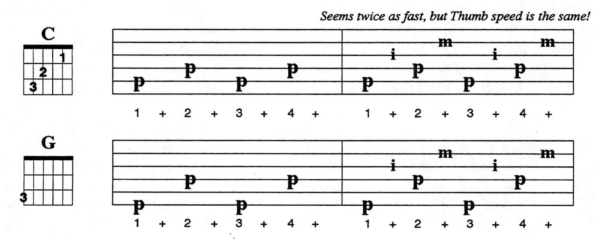

The measure that includes the fingers sounds ***busier*** than the one with the Thumb alone. Technically, the tempo is the same; it just *seems* twice as fast (double-time) because we're hearing Eighth Notes versus Quarter Notes. And remember to keep the rhythm dead even: rat-tat-tat-tat-tat-tat-tat-tat. People tend to get so wound up in playing the right finger sequence that they forget to keep the clock ticking.

(3) What do you do with the rest of the Picking Hand? In classical playing, they tell you not to rest your hand on the guitar, to keep the Picking Hand hovering over the strings. Well, I've seen some fabulous players who plant some portion of the hand on the instrument itself to create some stability. Here are some of the variations that can be seen in the wild:

(a) Set the Little finger on the front of the guitar just below the strings. (Not the **a** finger!)

(b) Rest the heel of the hand or wrist on the front of the guitar just above the strings or on the bridge. (This is easier if you use a thumbpick.) If you play an acoustic guitar, this may, regrettably, reduce the vibration of the wood and cut back on sound production.

(c) Keep the **a** finger planted on the 1st string. This is what I do, so it's probably ***illegal***, but it does give me a degree of stability, and when I *do* need to *play* the 1st string, I'm already locked and loaded. Just don't tell anybody I do this.

A more descriptive term for Travis #1 is the **Inside-Out Pattern**. This refers to the order in which the treble strings are played: the 3rd string first (Count 1+), which is closer to the "inside" of the neck, followed by the 2nd string (Count 2+).

So, I know that you're aching to practice the Inside-Out Pattern. Try this:

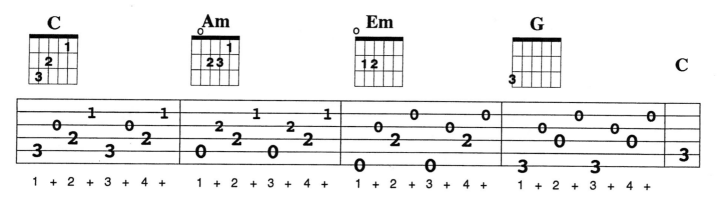

Pretty straightforward; **5/4** for a while, then **6/4**. *I'll continue the practice of showing you the 4 Thumb notes in each measure as **larger numbers** in the Tab Diagrams.* Now try the chords to the first part of the Verse for my version of Steve Goodman's "**City of New Orleans**."

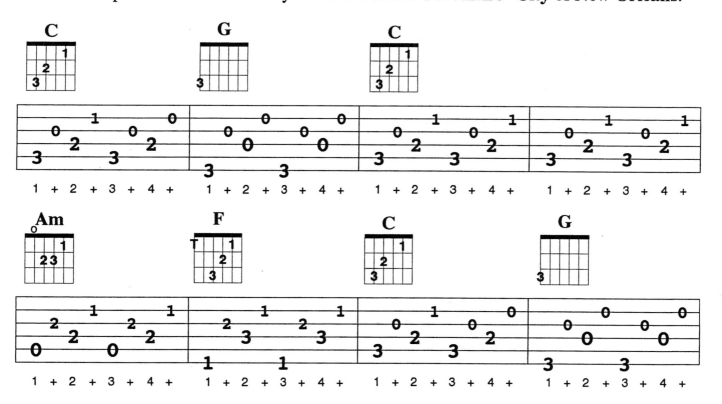

Go slow and steady. Did you notice the Escape Hatches from **C** to **G**?
And the 1st finger anchoring from the 3rd measure through the 7th measure?
All the usual tricks of the Fretting Hand still apply, the covering, the deception, the intrigue. The 2nd line keeps you busy as you go right from **5/4** to **6/4** to **5/4** to **6/4**. But it's all in a day's work for the Travis-Style Guitarist.

The **5/4** and **6/4** versions of the Inside-Out Pattern show up over 90% of the time, but some chords, like our friend the **D** chord, have 4th-string basses. So we'll create a **4/3** version by shifting the entire **5/4** version toward the floor (also known as "up") by a single string. On to the second part of the Verse to **"City of New Orleans"**:

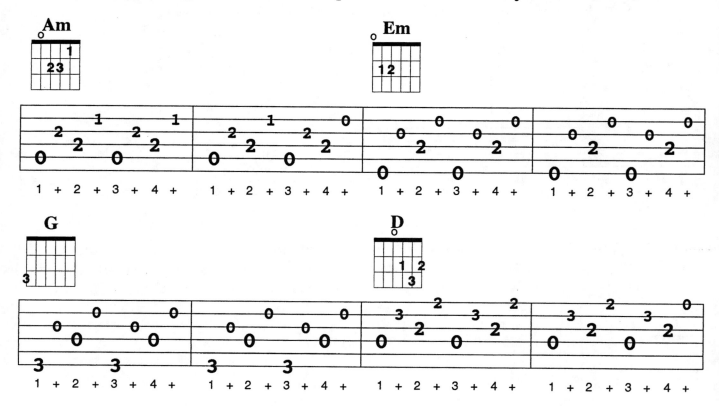

I'm just assuming that the very last note will be an Escape Hatch. Internally, the **4/3** pattern is identical to the **5/4** pattern, since there is no need in either one to skip over a string, as in the **6/4** pattern.

For those who love a challenge, let's take the chord progression from page 8. The good news is that the 1st finger remains as an Anchor through seven chords. The bad news is that the chords change twice as often, so you find yourself racing through *two chords per measure*. It's a quantum leap from the above passage.

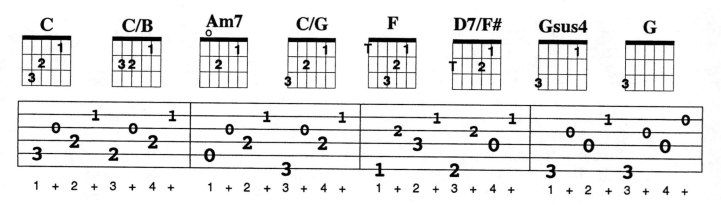

Notice the contorted fingering for the **C/B** chord. That's so you can keep both the 1st and 2nd fingers as Anchors for the first 4 chords.

Travis-Picking Repertory

Here's an alphabetical list of songs that either do, could or should use Travis-Style fingerpicking. Many of these songs will appear later as specific examples of different variations on the Alternating Bass style, but you can use Travis #1 for any of them:

Alice's Restaurant	*Going to California*	*Michelle*
Black Water	*Helplessly Hoping*	*Reason to Believe*
Can't Find My Way Home	*Homeward Bound*	*Souvenirs*
Cat's in the Cradle	*If I Had a Boat*	*Teach Your Children*
City of New Orleans	*If I Needed You*	*The Boxer*
Dear Prudence	*Landslide*	*The Dance*
Don't Think Twice	*Last Thing on My Mind*	*Will the Circle Be Unbroken*
Dust in the Wind	*Leader of the Band*	*You Are My Sunshine*
Freight Train	*Leather and Lace*	*You Were Meant For Me*
Garden Party	*Me and Bobby McGee*	*Take Me Home, Country Roads*

But now it's time to move on to *Travis #2*, the Truncated Inside-Out Pattern. Try it with **C**:

The only difference is that the very last note, the **m** on Count 4+, has been totally obliterated.

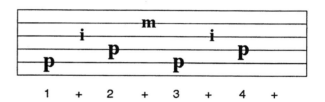

In and of itself, this is no big deal; you just stop a half-beat early with **p** on Count 4. But although the note is gone, the *time value* of the note remains, turning that last note into a Quarter Note and effectively inserting a pause at the end of the measure, a chance to take a musical breath.

This deletion should have no effect on the behavior of the Thumb, which must continue to alternate steadily, neither slowing nor quickening, just marking off the numbered counts. My ear likes that gap because it provides relief from the constant barrage of treble notes. ***Opportunities for artistic variation lie in the treble region, not in the bass.***

Try the Main Riff to "**Landslide**," by Fleetwood Mac:

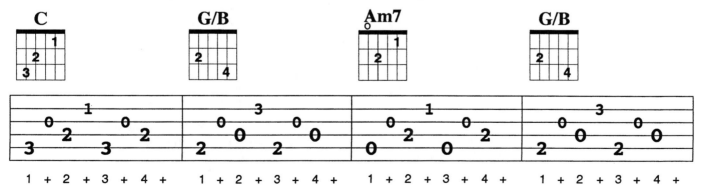

In the 2nd measure, be sure to use the 2nd and 4th fingers in the **G/B**; don't let that bully of a 1st finger push the 2nd finger aside. And in the same measure, you can wait a bit to add the 4th finger, which isn't needed until the boulder shows up at Count 2+. And there's no rush to grab the **Am7**, either.

It's always a good idea to try to sniff out any useful *patterns* that may exist in a given series of chords. In the "Landslide" riff, the 2nd finger finds itself in a continuous alternation between the 4th and 5th strings at the 2nd fret:

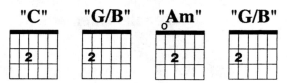

To me, just knowing this fact makes the whole thing seem easier. And the way it works with the guitar is, *if it seems easier, then it **is** easier!*

I don't know exactly why Lindsey Buckingham, the guitarist for Fleetwood Mac, decided to omit that final note in each measure. He may just have wanted to create some space.

But if you do fill in all 8 slots with notes and use an Escape Hatch on the last note, the open 2nd string, well, it just sounds lame, and you can't make me do it. And if you try to keep the chord in place until the bitter end, you have a significant Ping Problem with that last note in every measure, almost a pull-off to the open string. No, Lindsey and I think it sounds the cleanest with the pause.

"**Landslide**" is great for practicing Travis-Style because it stays **5/4**, repeating the same riff, all the way until the Bridge, when it finally switches to **6/4** for a bit. Here is that Bridge; it kicks in after an **Am7** chord, goes back to **C - G/B - Am7**, repeats *again* and then we return to the full Main Riff:

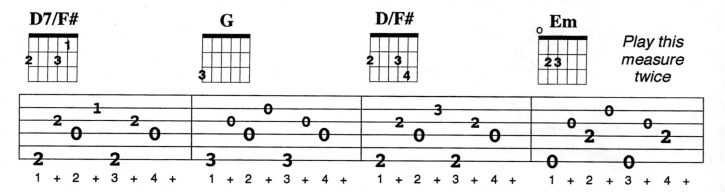

As we keep adding new patterns, feel free to swap them back and forth among different songs and mix them up within the same song. Each time you learn a new pattern, play it enough times in a row to become comfortable with it. Changing patterns means "waking up" the Picking Hand just enough to confirm that, yes, the Thumb is still doing its job while the fingers are learning something new.

Each new pattern will modify the behavior of the fingers, but not the Thumb. This may lead you to think that we're more interested in what the fingers are doing, that we care more about them, but no. What we are *really* doing is trying to establish the *independence of the Thumb,* so that it will completely ignore any kind of distraction that we might throw against it and just keep soldiering onward. "Hit me with your best shot," your Thumb will say, grinning maniacally. "Fire away."

And as you assimilate these patterns and switch them back and forth automatically, your fingers will start to behave like a team of horses, with you holding the reins. Each horse knows how to do its job, so you, as the driver, don't need to see when every hoof hits the ground. You just keep track of the changing landscape and steer the team along its way.

Since there is an Inside-Out Pattern, there must be an **Outside-In Pattern**:

We'll call this *Travis #3*.
Yep, same Thumb pattern, but now the more outside string (the 2nd) goes first and then comes the inside string.

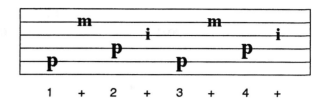

Here, try it on for size:

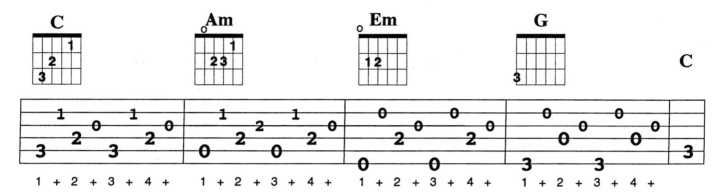

Now, I'm not trying to influence you *in the least*, but wouldn't you much rather play the Inside-Out than the Outside-In, huh, huh? Actually, there's hardly a dime's worth of difference between the two. I like the Inside-Out pattern for the simple-headed reason that it was the one I learned first. But really, once I get going playing one pattern versus the other, I can't tell them apart. Try each of them while holding the C chord:

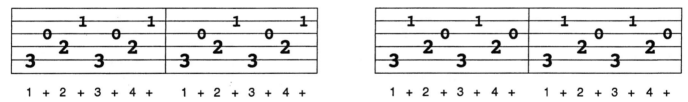

When offered an uncoerced choice, most of my students seem to prefer the Inside-Out. Maybe it does just feel a bit better in the hand, I don't know. Since you have started with the Inside-Out, it will naturally feel better than the Outside-In, but give the new one a fair shot, if only to challenge the Thumb a bit. You might like it better *(no-no-no)*.
Here's the (simplified) first line of Paul Simon's **"The Boxer"**:

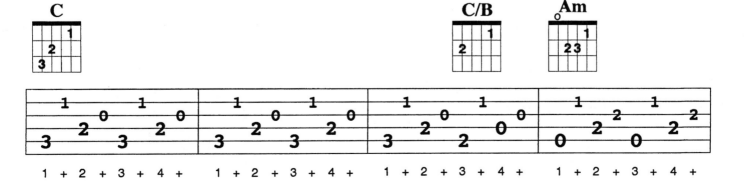

Outside-In Variations

While I am not really a fan of the straight Outside-In Pattern, there are definitely some variations on this pattern that send me right to My Happy Place. We'll be deleting notes and shifting them around and *everything*. And henceforth, most of our patterns will last an entire measure (4 beats) rather than a half measure (2 beats).

To play *Travis #4*, take the Outside-In Pattern and *omit* the first treble note, leaving a gap:

Now, this can be tricky: *Do **not** lose the even alternation of the Thumb.* Just because we left out a note doesn't mean we can ignore the amount of time it would have taken to play that note had we *not* left it out.

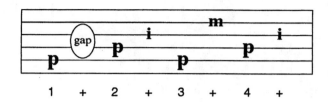

Upon first playing this pattern, people tend to rush the second Thumb note, compressing the measure. They play the 7 notes as if they are all Eighth Notes instead of 1 Quarter Note plus 6 Eighth Notes. This reckless behavior leads to a disturbing new meter, 7/8 Time:

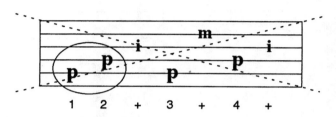

While 7/8 Time does indeed exist, it has no place between the covers of this book. *Drill:*

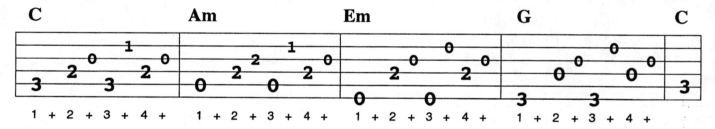

If you have trouble keeping that rock-steady bass, take the treble notes away and just work the Thumb for a while, then add the treble back. Just *breathe* after Count 1.

In the interests of further comfusing the Thumb, I give you *Travis #5*, in which yet another note is deleted, this time the last **i** on the 3rd string. Talk about Thumbal overuse! Try a (simplified) line from Harry Chapin's **"Cat's in the Cradle"**:

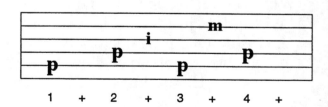

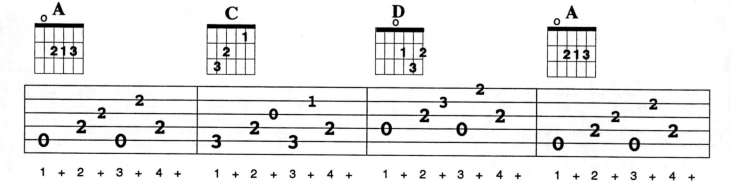

Picking Pattern Potpourri

Here's one possible way to string together four of our Travis patterns. Try it with **Am**:

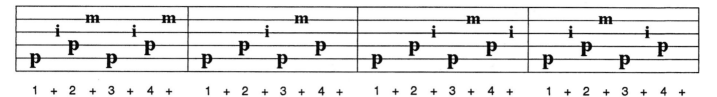

I'm not suggesting that you should be able to combine these patterns right now in random sequences at the same time that you're trying to remember the chord changes and learn the words to a song. That would be an overload. I bet most singer/players just stick with a couple of their favorite memorized patterns and that's about it.

But it might actually develop somewhere down the road that you'll be able to loosen the reins on that team of horses and let them run more freely. *As long as you keep the Thumb moving, you can't really make a mistake.* You can go out on a limb and try stuff like.....

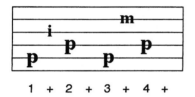 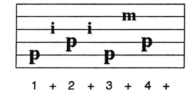 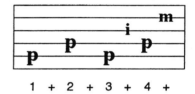

.....just whatever happens to come out. And you'll always have the automatic patterns you've already learned to fall back on. Here are the chords to the first eight measures of Bob Dylan's **"Don't Think Twice"** (but not the way he played it; he stuck with Travis #1 mostly). These are just random picking patterns I threw together:

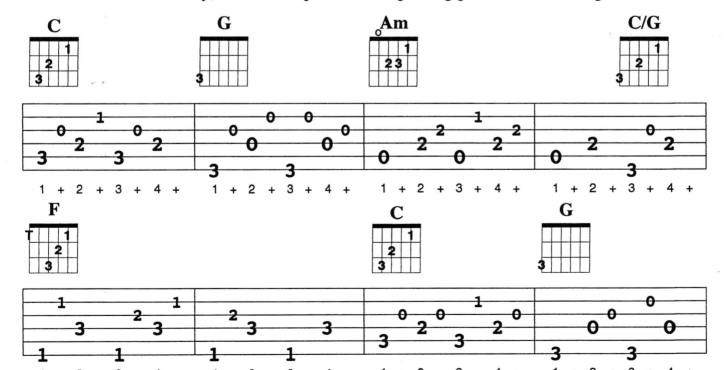

The Triple Alternating Bass Option

Let's add a Third Dimension to our Travis-Picking:

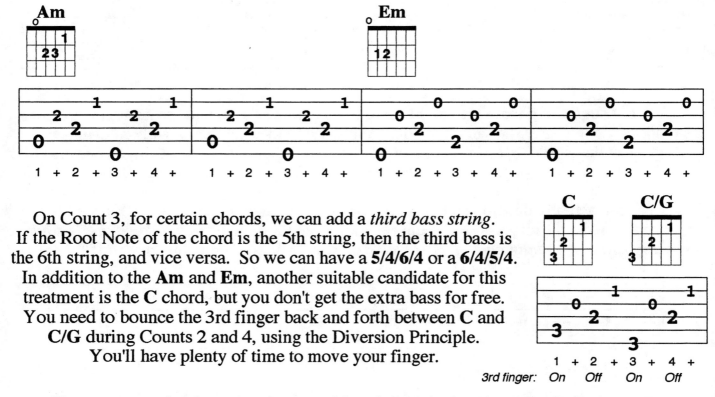

On Count 3, for certain chords, we can add a *third bass string*. If the Root Note of the chord is the 5th string, then the third bass is the 6th string, and vice versa. So we can have a **5/4/6/4** or a **6/4/5/4**. In addition to the **Am** and **Em**, another suitable candidate for this treatment is the C chord, but you don't get the extra bass for free. You need to bounce the 3rd finger back and forth between **C** and **C/G** during Counts 2 and 4, using the Diversion Principle. You'll have plenty of time to move your finger.

To me, many chords are not improved by tripling the bass, such as **G**, **F** and **D/F#**. But **A** and **E** work, and you can even do a **4/3/5/3** for the **D** chord, if you like. Here's a modification of the first two lines of "**City of New Orleans**":

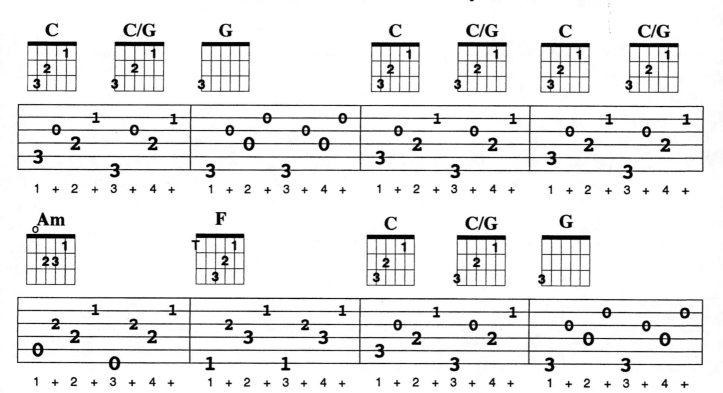

And these are the chords to the second part of the Verse of **"City of New Orleans"** that we saw earlier. I'll show you how to modify the **G** chord to have a Triple Alternating Bass (it's okay, I guess, but I don't bother to do it) and give the **D** chord the **4/3/5/3** pattern:

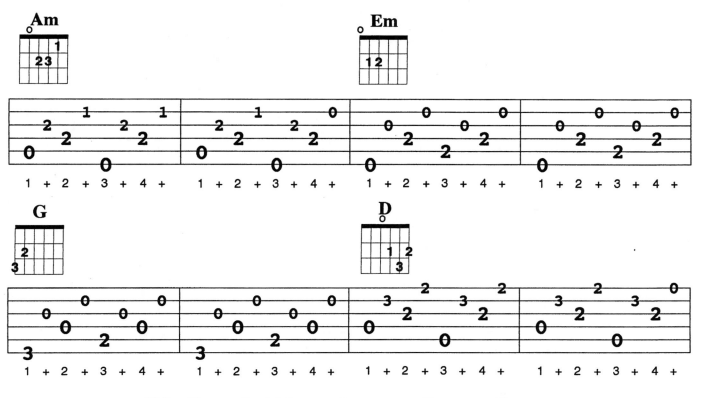

"The Boxer," which you also saw earlier, actually uses the Triple Alternating Bass over the Outside-In Pattern:

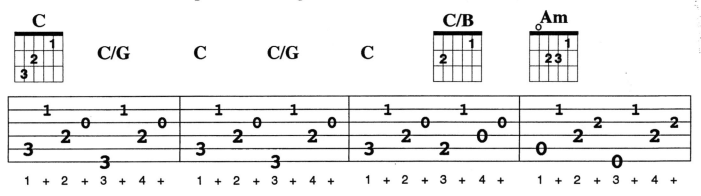

And here's the unsimplified (actual) 1st line of **"Cat's in the Cradle,"** using Travis #4:

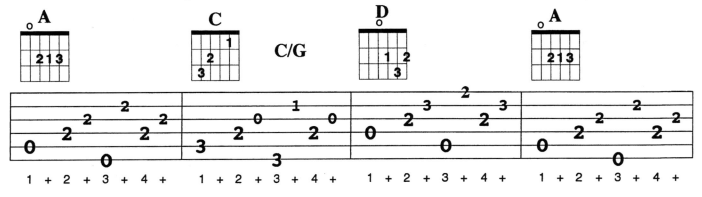

Walking Basslines

Now you'll get to see how to import Walking Basslines into Travis-Picking.

There's nothing esoteric about it; you just interrupt the picking pattern and insert a Walkup or a Walkdown in the bass to tie together the bass notes of successive chords. Let's try it with **"City of New Orleans"**:

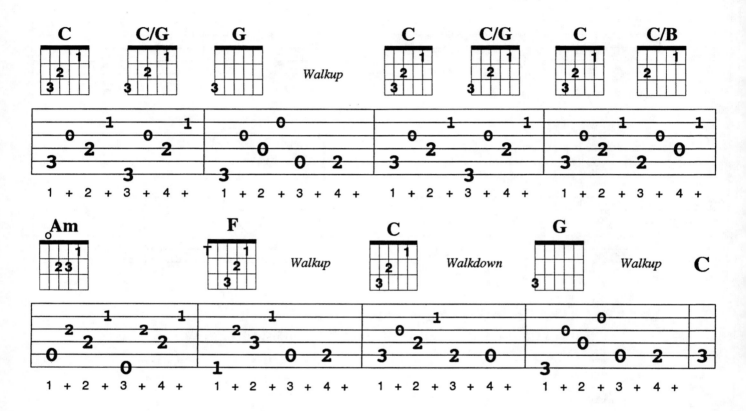

Be careful not to overuse this trick, as I believe I just did above.
The 1st line of the Chorus to **"Homeward Bound"** also works well,
and we can even stick in some extra treble notes to jazz it up a bit:

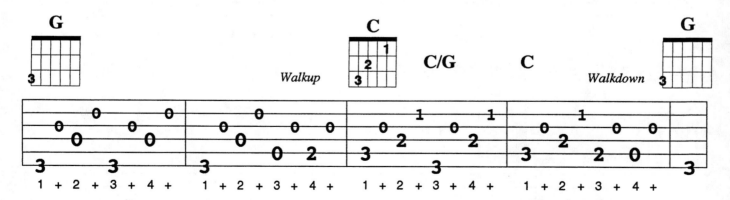

My students' eyes always light up when they see
these techniques, which turn out to be so simple to do.

The Travis-Style Pinch Pattern

This page marks the return of the **pinch**. So far in Travis-Picking, we have kept the treble notes on the offbeats ("+" counts) of the measure. *But when a treble note occurs right **on** the beat (a numbered count), it comes together with a bass note, simultaneously, resulting in a **pinching** motion between Thumb and finger.*

Introducing the pinch into Travis-Picking is a big step toward playing actual melodies over an alternating bassline, a bridge between playing accompaniment and playing solo. This is because most of the notes found in most simple melodies occur on the beat, while the offbeat is the domain of **syncopation** (intended, improvised or accidental).

Your First Travis-Style Pinch Pattern is a variation of the Outside-In Pattern, and already I regret having told you that, because they feel and sound so different. I want to show you the pattern in stages, starting with just the bassline and then adding the treble notes one at a time. There is more than the usual potential for throwing the Thumb into a tizzy, so let's go slow. Hold down a **C** chord, try the raw bassline alone (1), then add the pinch (2):

This isn't so awful. You start with 4 Quarter Notes and you end up with 4 Quarter Notes. Play **m** on the 2nd string opposite **p** on the 5th string for the pinch on Count 1. Just make sure that you keep that Thumb on track, alternating evenly and chugging along steadily throughout the measure.

(3) This is the part that may be disruptive, because when you add **i** on the 3rd string at Count 2+, you're creating an Eighth Note feeling that can spread like a virus and speed up everything. *But don't you let it happen,* particularly after the pinch. Stay on the beat. Keep that space open at Count 1+. Don't close the gap. (Something like this happened in Travis #4.)

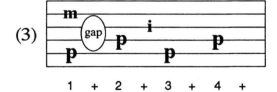

(4) Tossing another Eighth Note into the measure, the **m** at Count 3+, can further persuade the Thumb to jump in early after the pinch. You really, *really* need to keep the Thumb on track. Tick-tock.

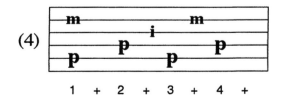

(5) A final Eighth Note at Count 4+ completes the pattern. Notice that we have one Quarter Note followed by 6 Eighth notes. If you repeat the pattern in rhythm, there's no gap between the last **i** note and the pinch, from Count 4+ to the next Count 1.

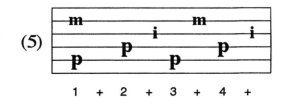

This, our first Travis pinch pattern, is *Travis #6*.
Compare it to the Outside-In Pattern, *Travis #3*:

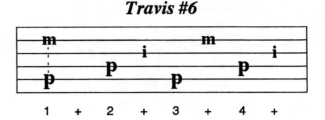

The only discrepency is the location of the first **m**, but that makes all the difference in the feel of the pattern. That pinch makes Travis #6 sound bolder, more definitive, almost forceful, compared to any of the non-pinch patterns. I consider Travis #6 to be a great little trooper, an Outside-In-with-a-pinch, while the Outside-In-*without*-a-pinch just leaves me in neutral. These are merely personal preferences.

I call this the "**Dust in the Wind**" pattern because.....that's what it is. I teach it all the time. Whenever the guys who work at the local music stores hear a customer playing "**Dust in the Wind**," they know the source. The Introduction is a great teaching tool, all **5/4** with minimal chord changing. Run through it first and then we'll discuss it:

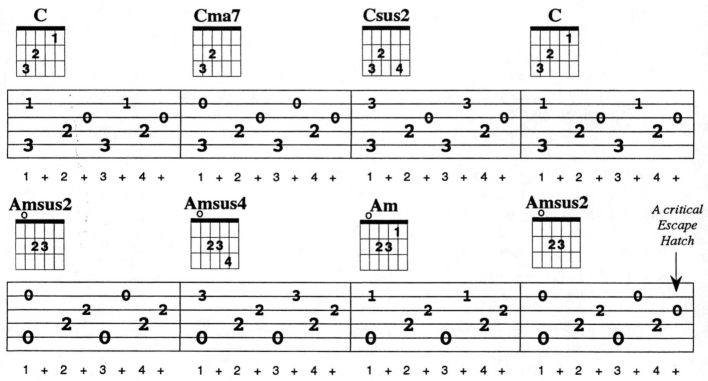

Continue with Travis #6, one measure per chord:

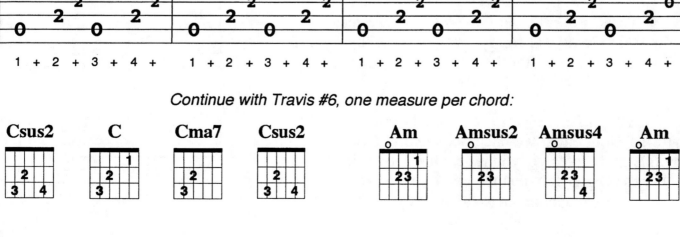

There may *seem* to be no rhyme nor reason to this chord progression, but there are some connections and patterns to be found. For example, the 2nd finger keeps the same note for the whole thing, all 16 measures. In fact, there's very little Fretting Hand movement from chord to chord.

Instead of getting hung up on all the **Amsus2/Cma7** chord nomenclature, consider that *there are only 2 chords*, **C** and **Am**, woven together with an embryonic "melody" line on the 2nd string. You play each chord for 4 measures, but the melody line is only 3 notes in length, C-B-D, or "1-0-3" on the 2nd line of the Tab.

Think of it this way: There are 2 overlapping cycles, one with a length of 3 measures and one with a length of 4 measures, and I call this *3 against 4*. We have 4 **C** chords, 4 **Am** chords, 4 **C** chords and 4 **Am** chords, but we only have *3 different melody notes* repeating, one per measure, putting us "out of phase" with the chord changes. That "1-0-3" sequence repeats independently of when the chords change. So keep on playing the 4 measures of each chord and keep going to the next note in the 3-note sequence. So if you play a measure with "1," then "0" is next. Play "0," and next comes "3." Then "3" leads back to "1."

Next comes the Verse, which starts off pleasantly enough with four more **5/4** chords, but then the kitchen heats up a bit. The next three chords are **G (6/4)**, **Dm7 (4/3)** and back to **Am (5/4)**. This is the Picking Hand equivalent of an 8-second Brahma bull ride:

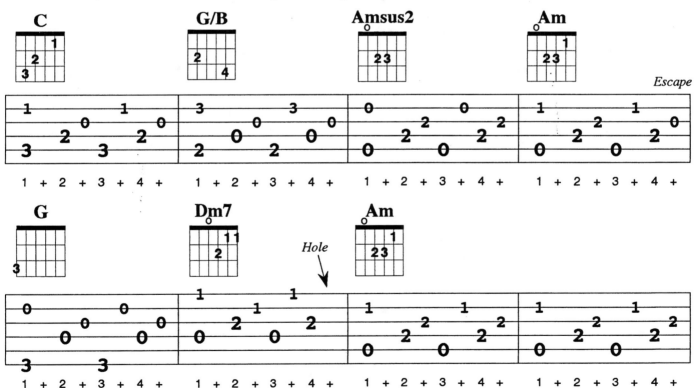

Most people make it to **G** okay; we really haven't practiced the **6/4** version of Travis #6 yet, and **G** would be an obvious candidate for such practice. But before you know it, you're darting off to the **4/3** pattern in the High-High Tier and then plunging back to earth with **Am**. I left Count 4+ of the **Dm7** measure empty (an Escape Hatch notehere sounds awkward) to give you a snowball's chance of getting back to **Am** in time.

Before going on to the Chorus, I want to show you some cute little variations. The first one occurs in the last measure of the Intro, leading into the first measure of the Verse. Instead of playing an entire measure of Travis #6, play the first half of it and finish the measure with *two separate pinches* on **Am** and **G/B**:

This gives a nice Walkup connecting **Am** and **C**.

Remember to observe the note values, whether Quarter or Eighth Notes, so that the bass stays dead even.

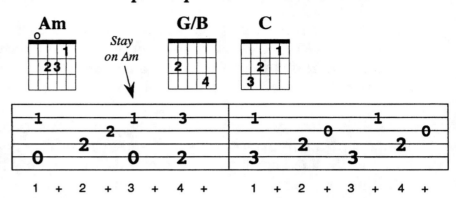

Try playing the 1st string with **a** in the 3rd measure, just once. (A portent of things to come.)

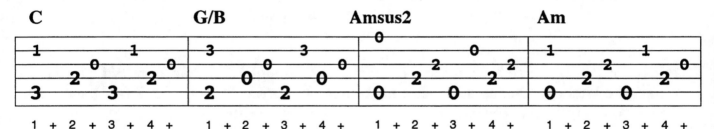

In the Chorus, there are more **6/4** chords to try. There's an Escape Hatch at the end of the **D/F#** measure that helps you avoid a Worst-Case Continuity Scenario. For **Am/G**, it's a stretch for the 4th finger, but it's okay to rest it on the unused 5th string. Then keep the 3rd finger anchored during the switch from **Am/G** to **D/F#** to serve as cover. *Then* there's a "**Blackbird**" sort of final measure, where the alternating bass drops away:

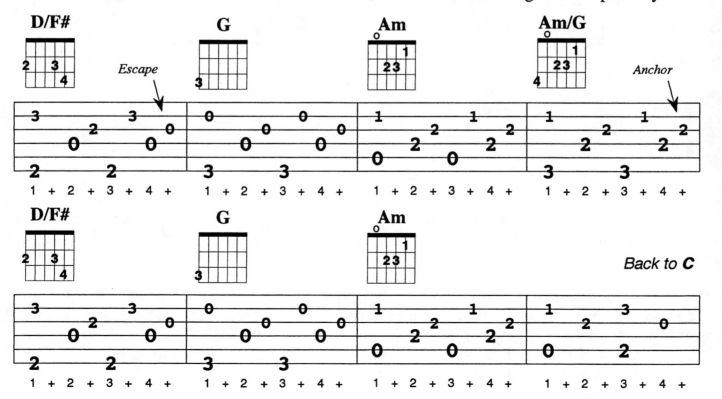

Back to **C**

You want the Bridge? You can't handle the Bridge! Actually, it's pretty simple. It's up the neck and 5/4:

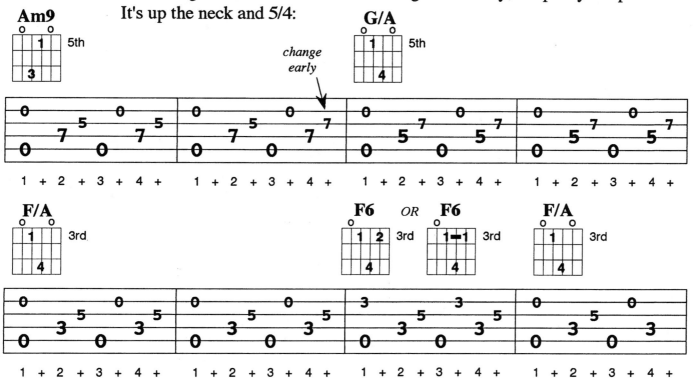

Something's happening here. We are accustomed to hearing higher notes on higher strings. That's what the term "higher strings" means: They contain notes that have higher pitches. But that's only true below the 5th fret. Once you get up the neck, it's very easy to find higher-pitched notes on lower strings. Look at the Tab:

The first note, B, the "0" on the 2nd string, has a slightly lower pitch than the second note, C, the "5," even though that C is on a lower string, the 3rd string. Anyway, this can throw off your ear a bit, since you would expect a note on a higher *string* to have a higher *pitch,* and most of the Bridge flies in the face of that expectation. I mention this because some people hear that discrepancy and try to "correct" for it by changing the pattern and playing the 3rd string first. But I guess YOU wouldn't do that, so excu-use me for even bringing it up.

As a teacher, I have found myself in the position of being asked to teach Travis #6 as someone's very first Travis pattern, without the benefit of the preliminary experience with the Alternating Bass that you've had here. If you find yourself in the same position, I've come up with a shortcut that seems to get people into it without too much trauma:

Concentrate on the Middle Four strings: Identify the Outside Pair (5th and 2nd strings) and the Inside Pair (4th and 3rd strings) of the Middle Four. The sequence you need to play is "Outside-Inside-Outside-Inside," with the first pair as a pinch and all the other pairs with the finger chasing the Thumb. Quick and dirty.

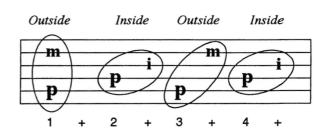

The song **"Brain Damage"** by Pink Floyd puts a nice spin on Travis #6. The fingers **i** and **m** stay in the *High-High Tier* and the Thumb maintains a Triple Alternating Bass that included the *3rd string*. There are several *huge* leaps between the 6th and 3rd strings. Let's just jump in the deep end and see if we don't sink:

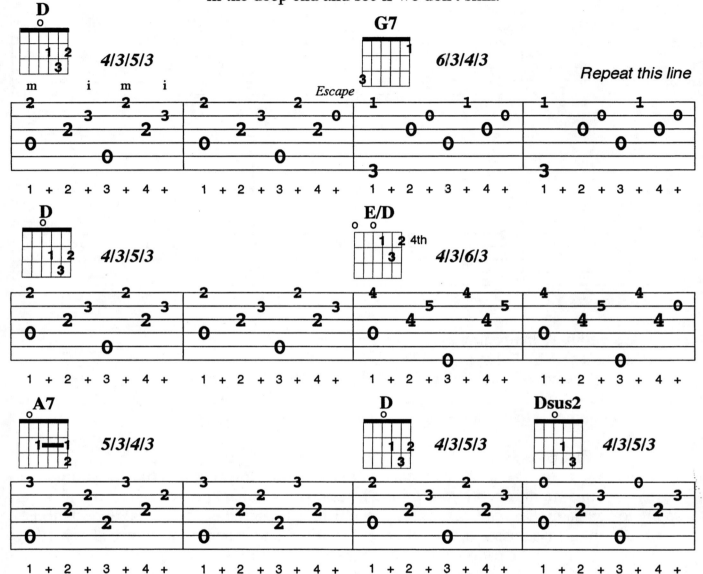

I know, it's freakish, especially that **E/D** chord. Leave it to those Floyds. Along the same lines, yet even more freakish, is *Travis #7*, the picking pattern to "Crazy Love," by Poco. Also played on the High-High Tier, this one can best be described as an **Inside-Out Pinch Pattern**. The **i** goes first! To my feeble brain, this does not compute, but it might work for you:

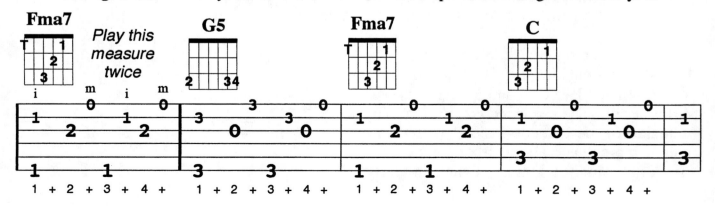

Let's see a different sort of pinch pattern, *Travis #8*, one where that hole at Count 1+ is filled in and a new hole appears at Count 4+:

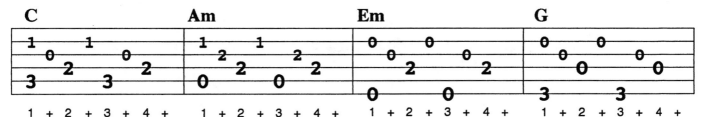

Not exciting enough? You could add **i** on the 3rd string at Count 4+ to fill in the new hole. *But you **may not** put **m** in that hole because then you would have two fast **m**s in a row (Counts 4+ and 1) and that would surely disrupt the rhythm.* There are certain limitations as to where the treble notes can go. Some things just don't work.

But there *is* a way to work in the **m** toward the end of Travis #8: Insert *another pinch* on Count 4 *(Travis #9)*. See if it doesn't sound to you like a Travis version of the **3/3/2** pattern. And why not *also* throw in the **i** at Count 4+ as suggested above? Getting pretty busy. Now it *really* sounds like a **3/3/2** pattern:

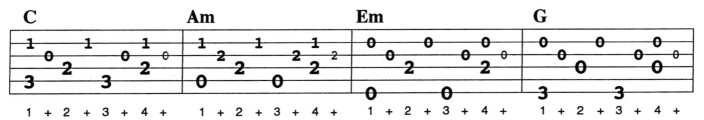

Maybe you're getting the idea that the number of possible Travis Patterns is limited only by your imagination, no? I will, of course, slog onward, giving you examples that I myself have run into, but don't let that stop you from experimenting on your own.

Let's transfer the pinch to the 2nd beat and call it *Travis #10:*

Travis #11 has pinches on both the 2nd and 3rd beats:

Let's hook two patterns together, Travis #10 and a modified Travis #8, this time with **m** in the hole:

63

Adding the Ring Finger

You knew this day would come, when that slacker **a** finger would finally be pressed into service. The party is OVER. In *Travis #12*, let's see how to incorporate **a** into the Inside-Out Pattern:

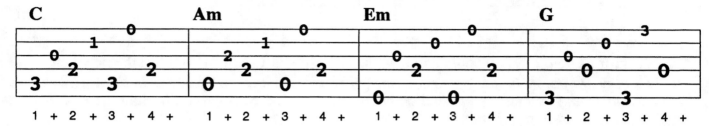

So what does your Thumb think about that? For many people, this alteration can be fairly challenging. The Thumb is way too distracted by this development and wants to flop around like a fish. Well, it's the same old process. You need to pull the Inside-Out Pattern back into your conscious thinking (put it back on the desktop), make the change and tinker with it until you smooth it out and your Thumb gets its mojo back. Then launch it back into the machine.

By adding a finger, we've increased exponentially the number of possible combinations of treble strings and the range of sounds you can produce. But I think you'll find, if you experiment, that not all the possibilities are truly *classic* or worth committing to memory. But feel free to scramble the notes around as much as you like in your musical quest. Meantime, I'll show you how some other players have fared with the Ring finger.

In the Intro to "**Burning Bridges**," by Garth Brooks (our *Travis #13*), you'll find the **a-m-i** sequence from Travis #12 shifted one beat later in the measure. It's an extension of Travis #4:

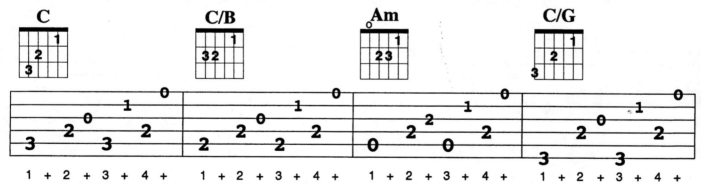

Travis #14 appears in the 2nd measure of the Chorus of Lyle Lovett's "**If I Had a Boat**." See how he mixes Travis Patterns #1, #3 and #4 in the last two measures:

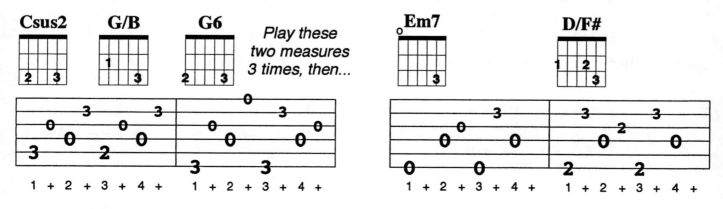

The following two patterns are played in **Drop D Tuning**. If you have an electronic tuner (ohpleaseohpleaseohplease), wind the 6th string down about one third of a turn and tune to the D note. In the absence of a tuner, go down the third of a turn and compare the note with the open 4th string, which is D, exactly one octave higher. The closer you are to being in tune, the slower is that beating sound you hear between the two notes, and when the beating goes away, you're there.

This is the Main Riff to the Beatles' "**Dear Prudence.**" John Lennon, who learned to Travis-Pick from Donovan, wrote this song about Mia Farrow. Or was it her sister? Anyway, leave it to John Lennon to rebel against everything we hold sacred by starting his Travis Pattern, our *Travis #15,* on *a bass note other than the D Root Note*. The bounder! But before we get our knickers in a twist, I think I know why he did it. He was trying to create a 4-note bassline on the 5th string (the A string, not the Root D string) and needed for us to hear those bassline notes right up front in each measure.

It's a **5/4/6/4** pattern all the way, but the Fretting Hand is tricky; there is some potential string muting, especially the open 4th string in the 2nd and 4th measures. You need to stand up the critical fingers (at the arrows) as straight as possible:

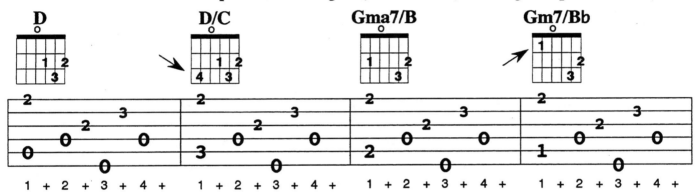

The part I really enjoy in this song is the Introduction. Play these chords using the same pattern, once through for each chord, except twice for the last C/D, and end on D. It starts high up the neck:

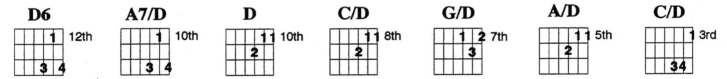

Here's the 1st line to "**The River**," by Garth Brooks *(Travis #16)*. The bass is steady, but oh, the treble. You've got two pinches in a row, and the second one, which I call a **tight pinch** (opposing **p** and **i**) bears out why we keep the Thumb positioned in front of the fingers......so that **p** and **i** don't ram each other during a tight pinch, that's why. I'll assume that you can now figure out which fingers play which strings on your own. Just stay in that Higher Tier and you'll be okay:

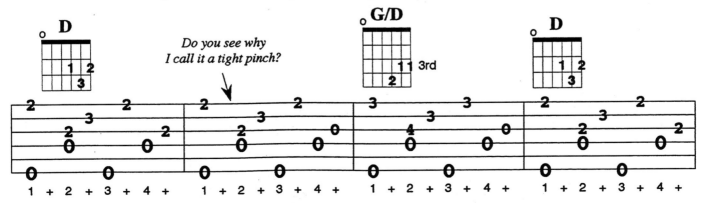

(In order to head off an unpleasant shock, retune your guitar to Standard Tuning.)

Travis #17 is how Lindsey Buckingham played the **"Landslide"** Main Riff in the 2nd Verse in a concert video in the 1990's. We have Anchor Fingers and a Pinch Pattern:

```
    Csus2           G/B             Am              G/B
```

```
───3───────3───────3───────3───────3───────3───────3───────3───
──3───────3───────3───────3───────1───────1───────3───────3───
────0───────0───────0───────0───────0───────0───────0───────0─
────────2───────2───────────0───────0───────2───────2─────────
──────2───────2───────0───────0───────2───────2───────0───────0
──3───────3───────2───────2───────0───────0───────2───────2───

1 + 2 + 3 + 4 +   1 + 2 + 3 + 4 +   1 + 2 + 3 + 4 +   1 + 2 + 3 + 4 +
```

He also devised an interesting pattern in the original version of **"Landslide"** from the 1970s, ***Travis #18***. I call this a ***3 against 4*** pattern, a term I recently used to describe the chord changes from measure to measure in the Intro to **"Dust in the Wind,"** but this time I'm talking about ***triplets within a measure of 4/4 Time.***

Recall that we talked about triplets in relation to the 3/3/2 Arpeggios, #19 and #20. There, we cut off the triplets at the end of the measure. Here, we allow the triplets to continue across the bar line and into the next measure. These triplets come at you relentlessly, occupying all eight slots and using 5 different pairs of strings for the 5 pinches in the two measures. Try this, if you dare (use a **C** chord):

This is the best exercise I can think of for trying to break up the dependence between the fingers and the Thumb. Try the Thumb alone, then the **a-m-i** triplet alone, then hook 'em up and hang on, pardner.

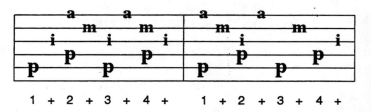

I still remember how I felt the first time I was able to keep separate track of the bass and treble at the same time. Wow. See the 5 distinct pinches distributed over the 3 triplets? They land on the following pairs of strings: 4/1...5/3...4/2...5/1...4/3. Of course, in the actual song "Landslide," there is a chord change at the bar line:

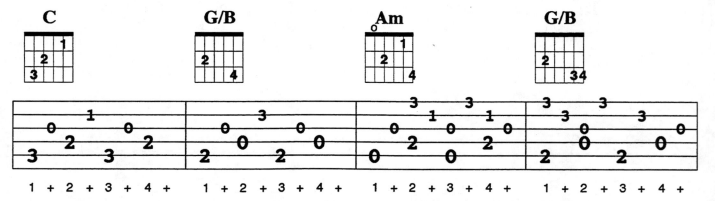

This is merely a variation of the Main Riff that we'd throw in once in a while for color.

If you thought *that* was a fistful of notes, try *Travis #19*, developed by
Jerry Reed, which he used in dozens of songs in the 1960s and 1970s. To me,
this is the Travis pattern that gets the closest to creating a Wall of Sound. It has
a Triple Alternating Bass with **i** and **m** *twinned* (odd), leaving **a** to fend for itself.
I have to *work* at it, even at a moderate tempo. It's like Travis #11 with **a** added:

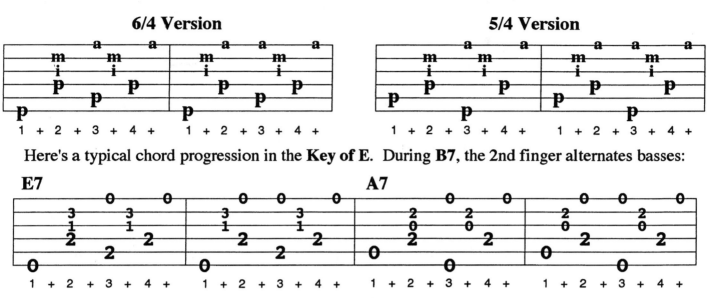

Here's a typical chord progression in the **Key of E**. During **B7**, the 2nd finger alternates basses:

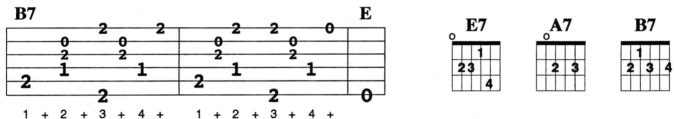

At the other end of the spectrum lies *Travis #20,* where the only treble notes in the whole measure
are front-loaded into a pinch on Count 1. This comes from "**Rebecca Lynn**," by Brian White:

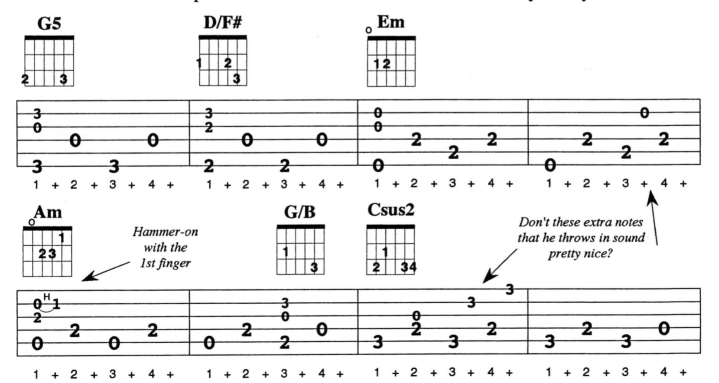

Hammer-on with the 1st finger

Don't these extra notes that he throws in sound pretty nice?

Twenty Travis Patterns: A Retrospective

It may seem oddly coincidental to you that there were *exactly* 20 Arpeggio Patterns and now there are *exactly* 20 Travis-Style Patterns in this book. It seems that way to me, too.

These are only the **5/4** versions of each pattern, just a stream-lined reminder.

More Samples From the Field

Let's keep poking around in the weeds, lifting various rocks and looking for little wriggles of Travis-Style genius. Let's go with Dan Fogelberg's **"Leader of the Band,"** which he wrote as a glowing testimonial and tribute to.....me. No, he wrote it about his father, which is nice and all, but I guess that's why I never hear anyone else sing it.

I want to leave the Intro for a bit later and start with a rather neat repeated lick from the Intro that is played out of a **G** chord and requires the Hammering-on of the 1st and 2nd fingers into a **C/G** shape. Take a look at it and then we'll talk about it:

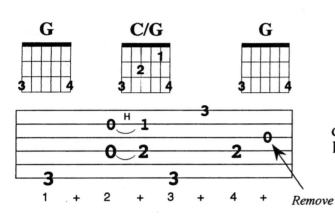

To get this bird to fly right, several things need to happen. First, the Hammer-on must be forceful and even. It's a **p-m** pinch on Count 2, *and don't rush it*. Tick-tock.

Then, *you must remove the 1st and 2nd fingers* at Count 4+ so that those two notes don't bleed over into the next measure. If you hang on to those notes and only remove those fingers in time to replace them on the next Hammer-on, it will never sound as if you have returned to **G**.

I'd recommend that you drill on the *second* half of the measure *separately* (Count 3 + 4 +). Hold the **C/G** and loop the 4-note phrase over and over and over, *then* hook it on to the first half.

Let's run through the whole song and see what treasures we may find. The main pattern is Travis #6, with a Triple Alternating Bass. First comes the Break and then the Verse:

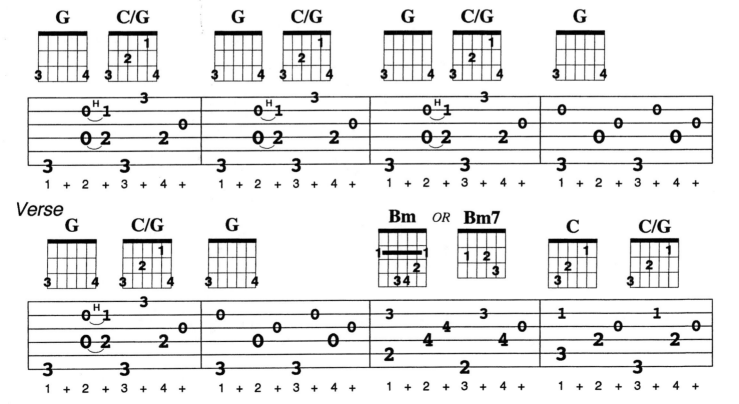

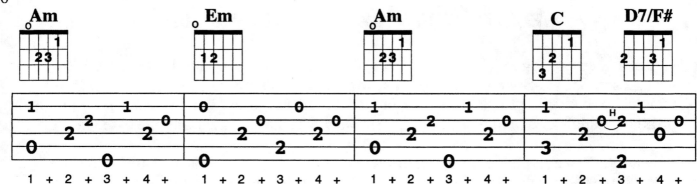

.....*Hold everything!* *We've had a significant chord change in the middle of a measure.*
This shouldn't faze the Picking Hand, but it probably will. Simply play a 5/4/6/4 pattern,
keep the 1st finger anchor, swing your 2nd and 3rd fingers around and grab the **D7/F#**.
It's not a pinch; you are Hammering-on the treble note while **picking** the bass note.
But hold off on the Hammer-on so that it comes *simultaneously* with the bass.

If you make the change with enough ***confidence***, the Hammer-on will occur naturally;
you won't have to force it, or even think about it. Dan Fogelberg may not even be aware
that he's playing a Hammer-on here; his right hand is so accustomed to minding its own
business that it just keeps rolling along regardless of what the fretting hand is doing.
It may be worth it to loop that measure, from C to D7/F#, over and over.
The Verse continues.....

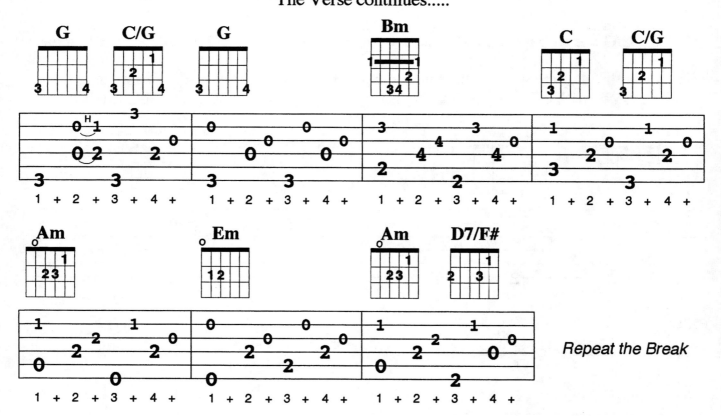

That last measure also has a major chord change right in the middle, but this time it's easier
to play; only the 2nd finger needs to move and there's no weird Hammer-on to worry about.

Play the Second Verse, this time skip the Break and go on to the Chorus on the next page.

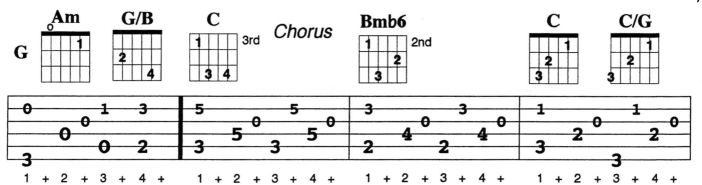

Whoa, I'm having a "**Blackbird**" moment with that **G-Am-G/B** move and then the 1st and 2nd chords of the Chorus. The 4th finger guides from **G/B** to **C**, then the 1st and 3rd fingers take over and guide to the **Bmb6**. If it helps with the switch from **C** to **Bmb6**, add the 2nd finger early, during **C**, just below the 4th finger. You won't hear that note anyway.

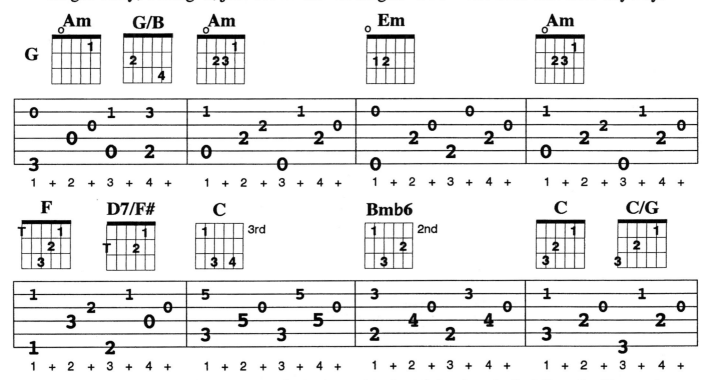

Notice the new fingering for **D7/F#**; since the thumb is already holding the F note in the bass in the previous chord, just slide it up one fret to F#. No Escape Hatch needed, but it is quite an alarming jump to the next **C** chord. Escape Hatch *definitely* needed.

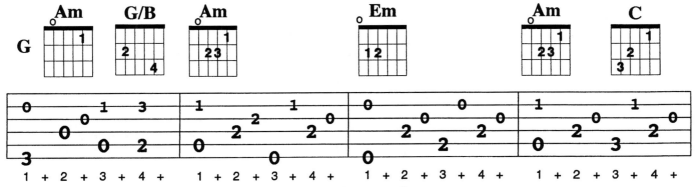

There's another chord change in mid-measure, an easy **Am** to **C**. Finish with the Break.

We'll return to "Leader of the Band" later to look at the more complex Intro. Now I'd like to show you the chords I use to play Rick Nelson's **"Garden Party."** There are many more mid-measure chord changes here, although they're not so daunting when you use our old friend, Travis #1. We did an exercise like this earlier, but now here's a whole song. Plus, I'll throw in some more Travis-Style fiddley-bits, and then we'll talk about them:

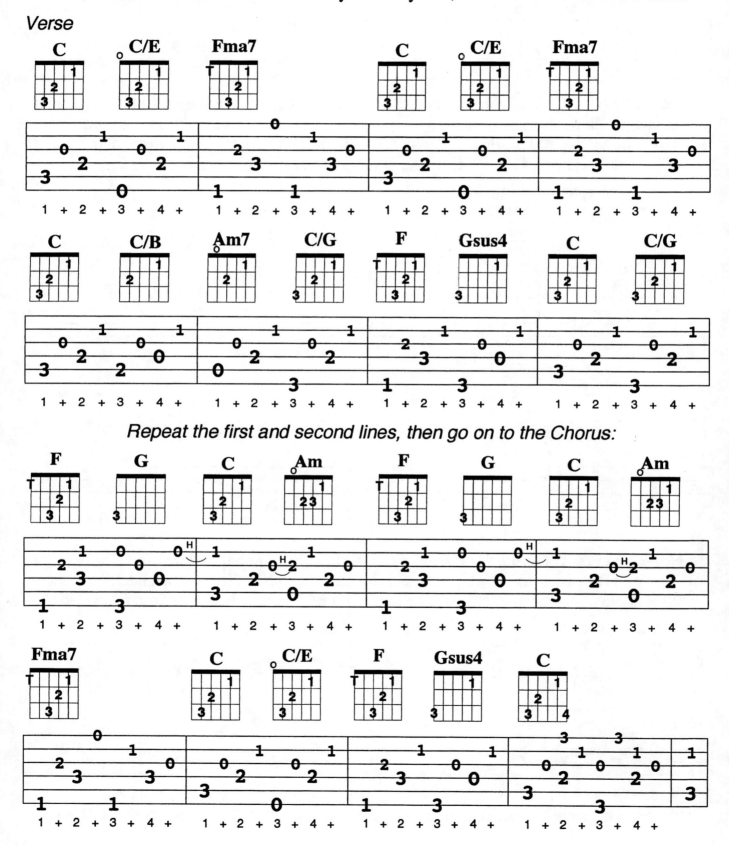

Repeat the first and second lines, then go on to the Chorus:

Comments:

(1) The 1st finger is proud to remain an Anchor Finger throughout the Verse.

(2) The reason for the **C/E** in the 1st measure is to get a little bassline going from C to **Fma7**, and the reason that it's an **Fma7** is that we're playing the open 1st string during this one-measure application of Travis #14.

(3) We get frisky in the Chorus. The 1st measure does a chord change halfway through this incarnation of Travis #11 (pinches on Counts 2 and 3). Then we have *two* instances, **C** and **Am**, of Hammer-ons that occur as by-products of forceful chord changes, like the one we saw in "Leader of the Band" from C to **D7/F#**. Don't *try* to do these Hammer-ons; just make the chord changes and *keep the Thumb moving*. If you do it right, the Hammer-ons occur simultaneously with the bass notes.

(4) There's even a piece of Travis #18, that "Landslide" 3-against-4 pattern, at the end.

- -

Moving on, here's an odd little critter from **"The Circus Left Town,"** by Eric Clapton. It stays up the neck, uses a few barre chords and has a two-measure pattern with pinches on Count 2 of the 1st measure and, similar to Travis #6, Count 1 of the 2nd measure.

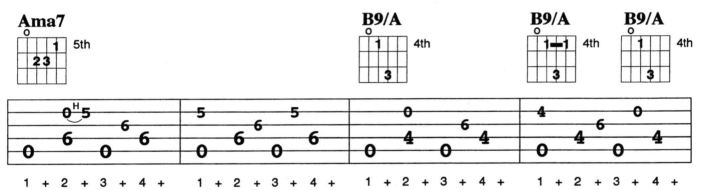

You have to start the **Ama7** with the 1st finger off and then Hammer-on the "5" in the pinch. The 3rd finger acts as an Anchor Finger into the **B9/A**, where the "6" is a higher note on a lower string, as we saw in "Dust in the Wind." You lay down a partial barre to get the "4" and then lift it off again just before you need the open 2nd string.

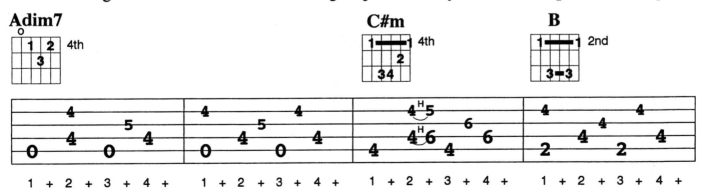

There's both an Anchor and a Guide Finger in the change from **B9/A** to **Adim7**. Then that "Hammer-on-to-the-barre" in the next measure is a bear. Put the barre down right away and then you have until Count 2+ to get into position for The Hammering.

Double-Picking

Double-Picking means that you pick the same string twice in a row, but with different fingers. This means that one of your fingers will need to go AWOL briefly and play a string other than the one to which it is assigned. In "**Helplessly Hoping**," by Crosby, Stills and Nash (and maybe Young; I'll check later), you see it quite a bit, mixed in with normal Travis-Picking. First, here are some *generic* ways that Double-Picking might arise.

Using the Inside-Out Pattern, the Thumb skips the 4th for the 3rd string on Count 2:

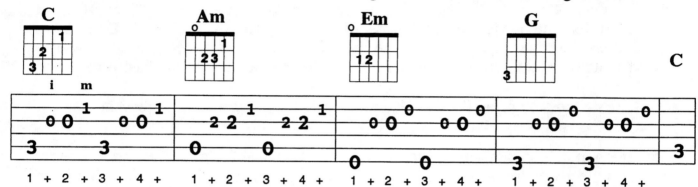

So the **p-i-p-m** sequence is maintained but the Thumb does a **5/3** bass pattern. Previously when we've seen the **5/3** pattern, the fingers have fled the Higher Tier and sought refuge in the *High-High* Tier, as in "Brain Damage;" but this time the fingers stay where they are.

And now it's the *Index finger* that intrudes on the *Thumb's* turf (Middle finger stays put):

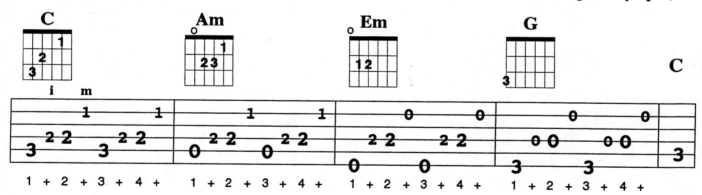

Then we go *simply mad* and move *both* the Index and Middle fingers bassward. The sequence is still **p-i-p-m**. It's as if you've compressed the Inside-Out Pattern from the usual 4 strings onto 3 strings. (This is classic a Leo Kottke move.)

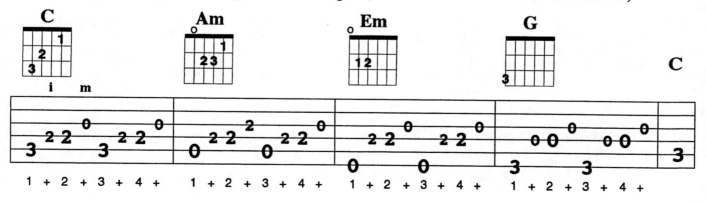

Seems we're getting more and more esoteric as we go. Well, that's what method books are 'sposed to do: go from the laughably simple to the mind-numbingly arcane. Try each new toy, and if you don't like it or it's over your head, turn the page. You won't hurt my feelings.

Back to CSNY's **Helplessly Hoping**." I think that whoever is playing the guitar part (either C or S, probably not N or Y) is doing a bang-up job. I mean, he's not bound to any particular pattern, but seems to delight in playing something a bit different in each measure. I've sorted out and laundered several passages from the Verse so that humans can try them.

This part sounds like "Leader of the Band"

Travis-Style Departures

Some songs have picking patterns that are not quite Travis-Style, but they're not quite *not* Travis-Style. For whatever reason, they don't maintain a steadily alternating, *boom-chick-boom-chick* bass throughout the measure.

The first such song that springs to mind is Jewel's **"You Were Meant For Me."** Here's the picking pattern from the Verse, without any Picking Hand markings:

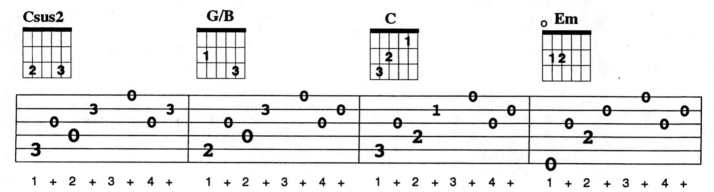

Well, what do you make of that? It starts out as an Inside-Out Pattern, with the expected bass pattern on Counts 1 and 2. But then the bassline falls to pieces, with *no note at all on Count 3* and a 3rd-string "bass" on Count 4. Here are two possibile ways I see to play it:

The first way is more intuitive for me. You play the first Inside-Out and *keep your fingers in the Higher Tier*. Let it breathe at Count 3 and finish with the **a**-**i**-**m** sequence.

The second way uses the gap at Count 3 to shift the whole hand into the High-High Tier so that the Thumb gets one more shot at a "bass" note on Count 4.

Me, I'd sacrifice the power of the Thumb on Count 4 in order to keep my hand from bouncing back and forth between tiers. I don't know what Jewel herself does.

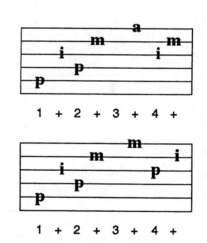

- -

Hey, is there a Travis-Style Pattern for **3/4 Time**? Try this:

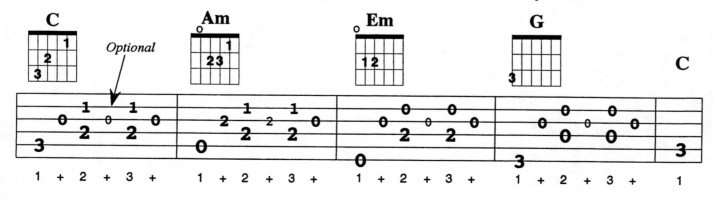

Hey, that works!

The Picking Pattern for "**The Dance,**" by Garth Brooks is a funny composite: The first *half* of the measure is a normal arpeggio, **p-i-m-a**, and the second half is Travis-Style with the Thumb playing on Counts 3 and 4. Here you do need to switch the fingers back and forth between the Lower and Higher Tiers in each measure that this occurs. You don't play the **D** chords Travis-Style at all here.

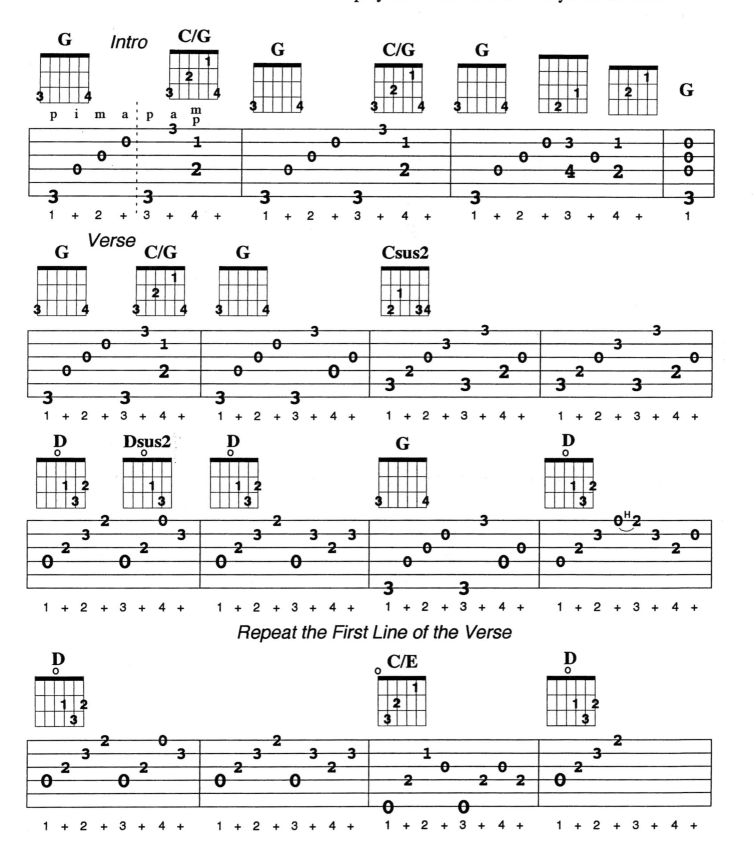

Blackbird Complete

Paul McCartney didn't Travis-pick "Blackbird," but I've adapted it to a sort of *quasi*-Travis-Style. The original arrangement contains these little pinch-and-strum strokes that I'm not entirely convinced that I understand. My version of it uses what I call "Alternating Bass Without the Alternating Bass."

I use two types of patterns: ***Arpeggio #7*** (the same pinch pattern as in the original) plus a *modified version of **Travis #6*** (from "Dust in the Wind"). Compare them:

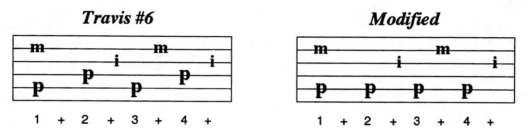

Because of the strange types of chords employed in the song, you don't really want to play the 4th string, and that's a problem when you have either a **5/4** or **6/4** picking pattern! So we simply don't alternate to the 4th string, resulting in a ***Non-Alternating Bass***.

I *would* strive to play it the way Paul McCartney plays it if I thought it sounded better, but he switches between "picking" measures (pinches) and largely "strumming" measures. To me, the transition is jarring. My way, it's all picking and no strumming, and since most of my students have also liked it, I have no reason to promote authenticity.

Here's the Introduction, which, when repeated, also serves as the first line of the Verse:

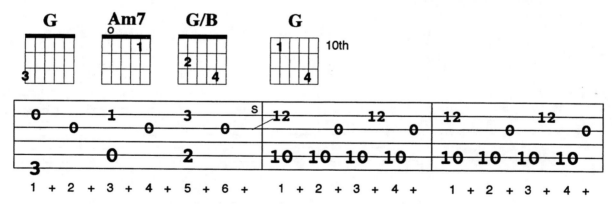

We start with some lovely one-finger chords. By the way, *G is the only chord in the song that has a 6th-string bass*, and once you move into the Verse, you won't play **G** again until the *end* of the Verse. (Watch that you don't play the open 6th string in **Am7**.) Later, you'll also run into one 4th-string bass chord (a **D7**-type), but all the remaining chords have 5th-string basses. That'll help a lot.

Be sure to use the 4th finger in G/B. *Once you've set down that 4th finger, it continues to act as either an Anchor or a Guide Finger throughout most of the Verse*. Slide it to the 12th fret and bring in the 1st finger at the 10th fret for the unusual **G** chord. And you'll need to work on that picking pattern (usually played once per chord, but twice here.)

So we've already seen both types of Picking Hand patterns. We have what I'll simply call, just for the purposes of this song, *the Pinch Pattern* and *the Picking Pattern*. And know this: **The sole responsibility of the Index Finger in this song is to play the open 3rd string (G).** This is true for both the Pinch Patterns and the Picking Patterns. That'll also help a lot.

Furthermore, there are what I consider to be two types of "chords-up-the-neck" in this song: Wide-shape and Narrow-shape chords. The Wide-shape chord spans 3 frets (the **G** chord at the 10th fret) and the Narrow-shape spans only 2 frets (the **G/B**). The Wide-shape ought to be formed with the 1st and 4th fingers (1st and 3rd is too wide a stretch), while the Narrow-shape will use either the 1st and 3rd fingers or the 2nd and 4th fingers.

As long as we're analyzing, Pinch Patterns are composed of Quarter Notes while Picking Patterns contain mostly Eighth Notes, so we'll get a busier, *double-time* sound from playing the Picking Patterns. Keep those Picking Patterns moving and drop to half-speed on the Pinch Patterns. Tick-tock.

Gather 'round as I relate the fascinating story of how I learned "**Blackbird**".....wrong. Odds are very good that, if you yourself have "learned" the song already, you've got at least some of it wrong, too. This has been my experience as a teacher, anyway. Here's how I learned to play the next part of the Verse from some guy down the hall at the University of Maine in 1979. Try it, but do not commit it to memory:

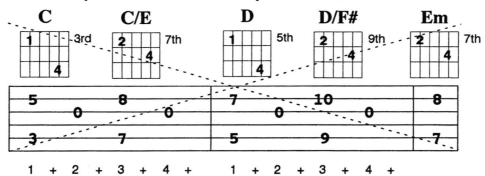

Well, that was how everyone did it, it seemed to work okay and I was thrilled that I was playing a truly *happening* song after several years of classical guitar lessons. Fast-forward three years. I was working for the U. S. Forest Service in Oregon and went visiting in the city of Bend, where my host owned a copy of the *White Album*. So I put the "record" on the "turntable," set the "needle" and was horrified at what I heard. Clearly, Paul McCartney had *not* learned "**Blackbird**" from the guy down the hall.

The melody notes sounded like mine, but the bass notes rose steadily in pitch, one fret at a time. So, keeping the melody and adding the so-called **chromatic** bassline led to the following:

I don't care *what* universe you live in, that's quite a stretch. I thought, That's just too uncomfortable. Then, using the power of the brain God gave me, I realized, Oh look, I have **another string!** It's called the *1st string* and it sits right next to the 2nd string! So I was able to move those two stretchy notes at the 8th and 10th frets of the 2nd string to **unison positions** (same notes) on the 3rd and 5th frets of the 1st string:

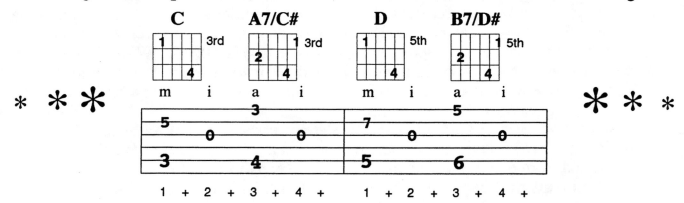

That had to be it. Plus, years later, I saw The Man Himself playing The Song Itself on an edition of *MTV Unplugged,* and darned if he didn't do it just the same as me! But left-handed. Of course, I still couldn't really discern how he gets those little pinching-strumming strokes. Maybe there needs to be *some* mystery in life.

Let's talk about the mechanics of the above two measures, perhaps the most eloquent passage in the whole song. Form the **C** chord and keep your 4th finger anchored as you swing the 1st finger around to grab the note on the 1st string and lay the 2nd finger down on the 5th string (**A7/C#**). Here, the 4th finger holds a string that isn't actually played.

As to the Picking Hand, this passage will be *the only opportunity in the song for* **a** *to play.* Use that Ring Finger to pick the 1st string. Then....**don't let your Middle Finger proceed to play the 2nd string on Count 4**. It will want to; everyone's does. *But don't you let it.* Count 4 is reserved for the Index Finger to do the only thing we allow *it* to do in this song, which is to **play the open 3rd string**.

If you can do the first measure, you can certainly do the second measure, *since it's the same fingering 2 frets up.* Use the 4th finger to slide to the 7th fret, swing the 1st finger back to the 5th string for **D** and proceed to **B7/D#**.

Note: I've been showing you no more than several measures of this piece at a time. Well, that's the way you should be learning something hard like this, several measures at a time. There's no virtue in playing through the whole piece badly, over and over. Polish each bit as you go, repeating from the beginning often. Don't make me beg.

After those four Pinch Patterns above, we have two measures of Picking Patterns. Basically, whenever you see two chords in a measure, you'll play *two Pinches*. If there is only one chord, as is the case here, you'll play *one Picking Pattern*.

Loop these chords over and over to practice the modified Travis Pattern.

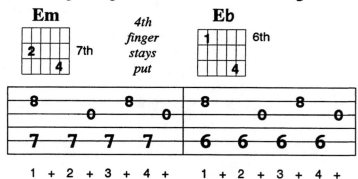

Now we come to the trickiest measure in the whole song. We've reached "the top" and now we're heading back down, really just retracing our steps:

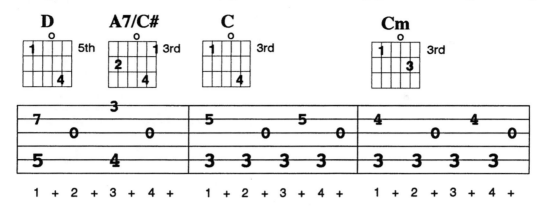

Do a Pinch Pattern on the Wide-shape **D** chord, *slide down 2 frets with the 4th finger guiding while swinging the 1st finger around to the 1st string and adding the 2nd finger to the 5th string.* Do a Pinch Pattern using **a**. Now keep the 4th finger Anchored while swinging back into the Wide-shape **C** chord and proceeding with a Picking Pattern. And look! You can finally give the 4th finger a breather during the Picking Pattern on **Cm**, a Narrow-shape.

So far, so good? Really, don't go on unless you can slowly, smoothly piece together everything we've already done. The last 4 measures contain all Picking Patterns. Here comes that 4th-string **D7** chord; the Picking Pattern will feel cramped, but there's enough room to fit it all in. Then it's back to the 6th-string **G** chord. Back to the Wellspring:

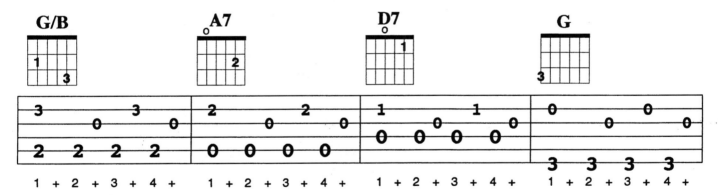

Then there's a little Tag Ending that comes after the First Verse:

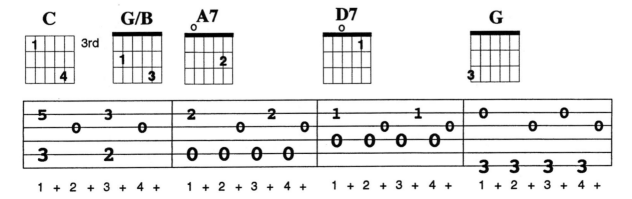

Start the Second Verse from that Intro line, and this time when you finish, skip the Tag Ending.

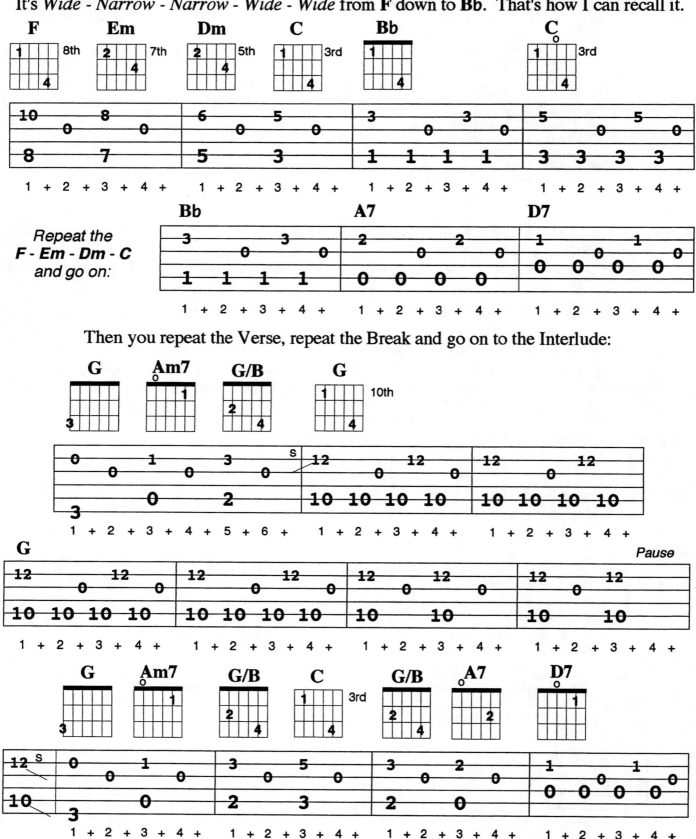

Bruce Emery's Own Extended Ending to Blackbird

I always feel like getting in *one more run* up and down the neck. A victory lap, if you will. You saw this chord sequence before in an example of Arpeggio #4, but now there are Pinches, too:

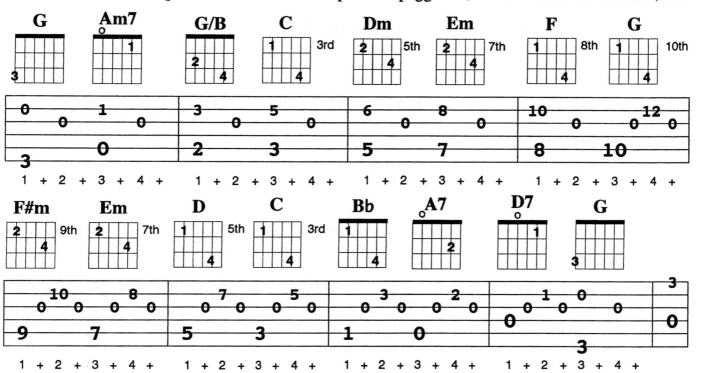

Actually, my ending was inspired by **Kenny Rankin's version of "Blackbird"** from 1974. I realize that the above arrangement is sort of pseudo-Travis, and that Kenny Rankin's version isn't Travis at all, but I wanted you to see what he did and this is as good a place as any for it. The 1st line is the Intro and the 2nd line starts the Verse. Notice: In place of the usual two measures of Picking Pattern at the 10th fret, he does 4 descending chords. Nice. That's the part I stole for my ending, and I play those 4 chords as Pinch Patterns in my own version.

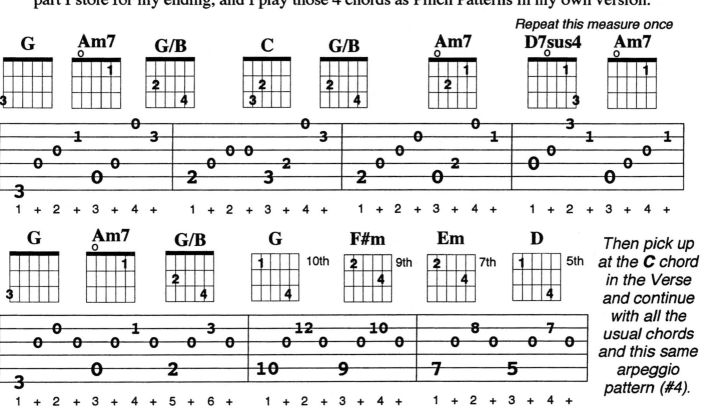

84

I can't help it. I need to show you more of Kenny Rankin's "Blackbird."
You know, some people at the time who had no familiarity with the Beatles' version thought that Kenny Rankin had originated the song. True, these people were probably living together in a cave along the Aegean coastline, spearing fish and rediscovering fire and the wheel, but that's not the point. Actually, there is no point. It's just nice, what he did with the song. Here are the chords to Verse Two, with Arpeggio #13:

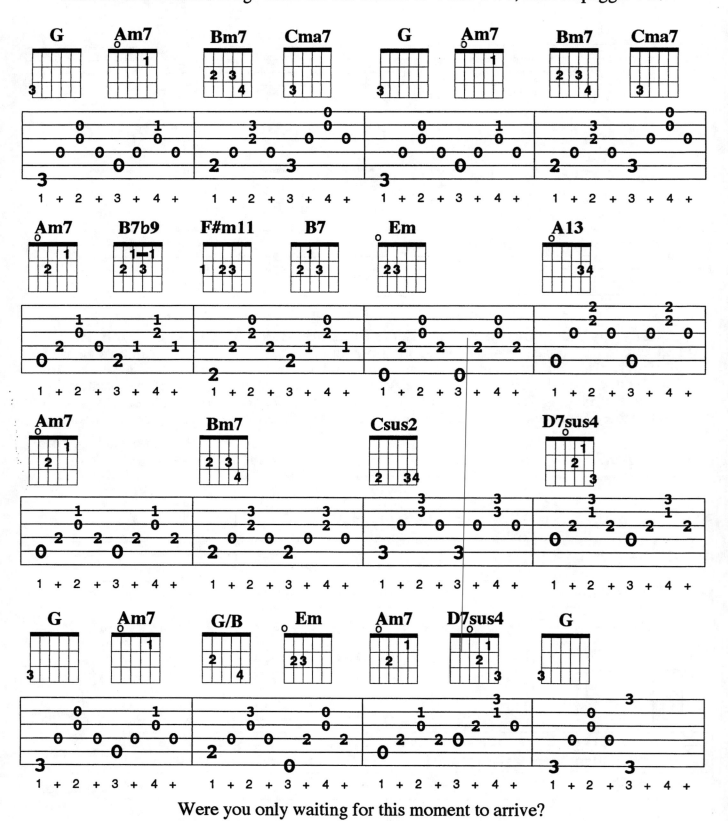

Were you only waiting for this moment to arrive?

The Next Level: Melodic Lines

Incorporating melodic lines into a Picking Pattern is the next step on the way to playing Solo Fingerstyle Guitar, where a melody, bass and harmony are all spewed out at once. We're at the point where we *hope* that the Alternating Bass technique has made a nest somewhere in your brain. The Thumb must operate independently while the fingers shun any kind of patterned playing so they can pick out these melodic lines.

Here's the Intro to "**Leader of the Band**." The 1st measure has a straight picking pattern, Travis #6, no problem, but in the 2nd measure, all those notes you see in the treble are part of the *melodic line*. After the pinch between the 5th and 1st strings (using **a**), the next 3 notes all occur on the same string, all on "and" counts, and you might as well use **m** to play all of them. This might singe your noodle a bit; you're not accustomed to playing *the same string 3 times in a row as the Fretting Hand visits 3 different frets and the Thumb struggles to maintain that strictly alternating bass.*

The 3rd measure is another Travis #6, but the 4th measure has another melodic line, again played mostly with **m**, both on the beat, as pinches, and off the beat. The 5th and 6th measure have melodic elements, too, but they play a little easier, and the last measure is a straight Travis #6. Off you go:

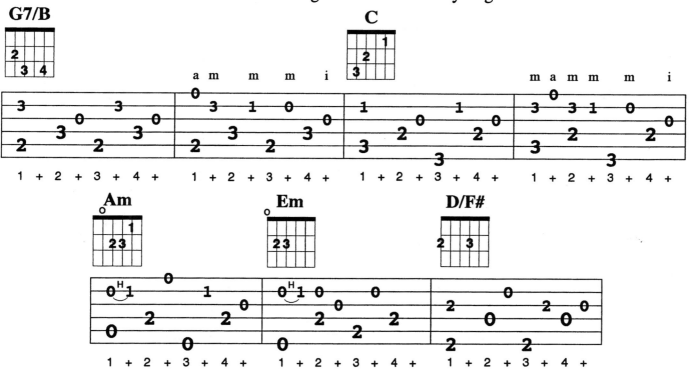

For another example, here's the Intro to "**Cat's in the Cradle**." Put a capo at the 7th fret the way he did, if you like. Use the 3rd finger for the melodic line in the 2nd measure:

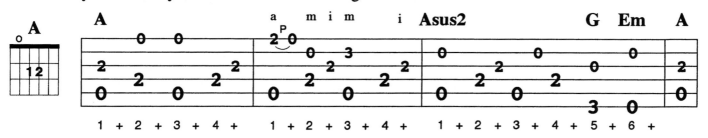

Those two melodic lines belong to introductions to songs. But you can also weave little melodies into the picking patterns that accompany *lyrics*. I call your attention to two Variations on the Main Riff in the live version of **"Landslide."** Of course, Lindsey Buckingham is not singing at the same time that he plays these things (Stevie Nicks is), so he can afford to devote more of his attention to creating diversity and interest.

Below, in the 3rd measure, there are pinches on Counts 2, 3 and 4; hectic but not hard. The next two melodic notes (in italics) occur on the "and" counts and on the same string, and they feel as if they anticipate the bass notes that come right after them (dashed lines):

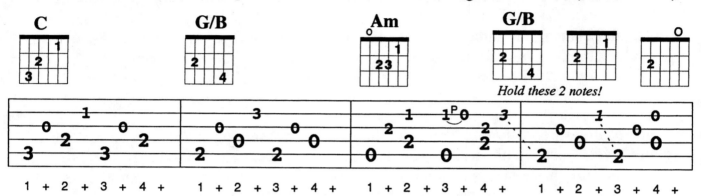

The next line is like the previous line, only more so. This time, you need to navigate back and forth between the 1st and 2nd strings using **a** and **m**, while the Fretting Hand does its thing. The last note, the open E string, should be kept ringing over into the C chord that would follow. All four of these melodic notes start between the beats and continue over the top of the following beats, and that's the definition of **syncopation**. If only the naming process made it any easier to do:

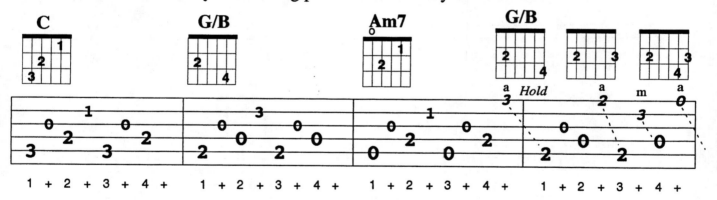

Can Travis-Picking get any more complicated than *this*? Oh, uh-huh. But that is for another day. I just wanted to set you on your way. But all this picking pattern stuff we've been doing has well prepared you for any Solo Travis-Style playing that you might want to get into someday, either through one of my future books or somebody else's. Here's a little scale exercise on a **G** chord, a quick peek into the future:

Fingerstyle Final Exam

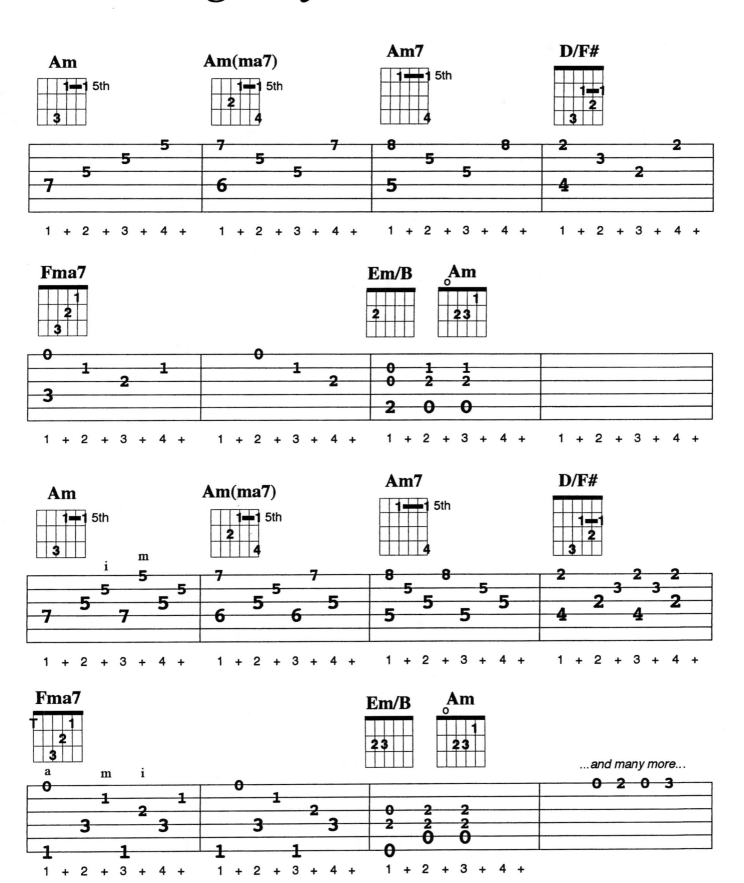

Our Twenty Arpeggios at a Glance

I thought it might be useful to present these two pages again here at the end of the book so you can flip it open and have immediate access to 40 Picking Patterns at a glance.

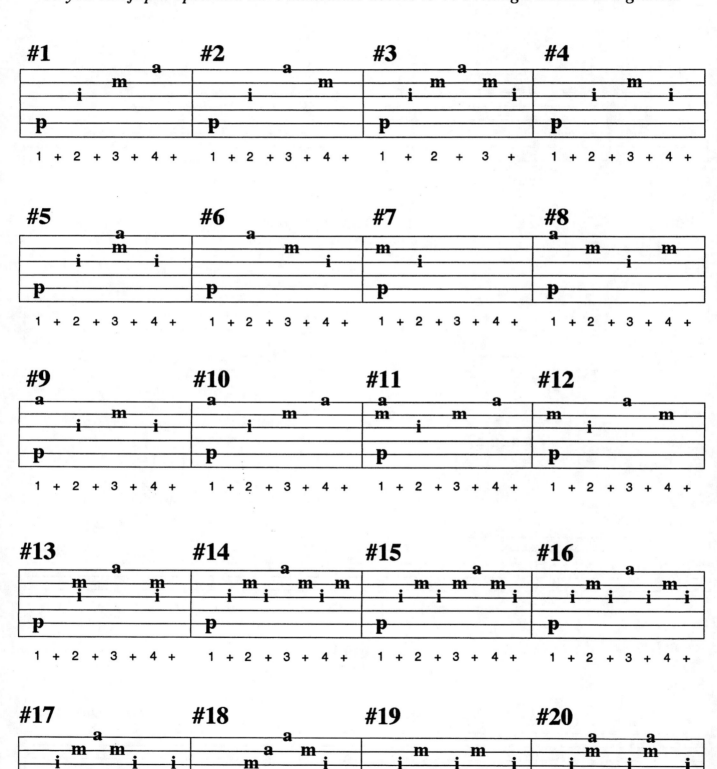

Our Twenty Travis Patterns at a Glance

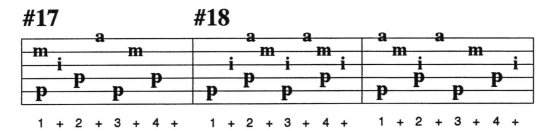
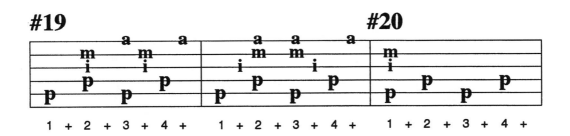